501
Sentence Completion Questions

501

Sentence Completion Questions

LearningExpress ®

NEW YORK

Library of Congress Cataliging-in-Publication Data:
501 sentence completion questions.—1st ed.
     p.m.
     ISBN 1–57685–511–2 (pbk.: alk. paper)
   1. English language—Examinations—Study guides. 2. English language—Sentences—
Problems, exercises, etc. I. Title: Five hundred one sentence completion questions. II.
Title: Five hundred and one sentence completion questions. III. Series: LearningExpress
(Organization)
LB1631.5.A17 2004
428.1'076—dc22   2003027067

Printed in the United States of America

9 8 7 6 5 4 3 2 1

First Edition

ISBN 1-57685-511-2

For more information or to place an order, contact LearningExpress at:
    55 Broadway
    8th floor
    New York, NY 10006

Or visit us at:
    www.learnatest.com

The LearningExpress Skill Builder in Focus Writing Team is comprised of experts in test preparation, as well as educators and teachers who specialize in language arts and math.

LearningExpress Skill Builder in Focus Writing Team

Lara Bohlke
Middle School Math Teacher, Grade 8
Dodd Middle School
Cheshire, Connecticut

Elizabeth Chesla
English Instructor
Coordinator of Technical and Professional Communication Program
Polytechnic University, Brooklyn
South Orange, New Jersey

Brigit Dermott
Freelance Writer
English Tutor, New York Cares
New York, New York

Darren Dunn
English Teacher
Riverhead School District
Riverhead, New York

Barbara Fine
English Instructor
Secondary Reading Specialist
Setauket, New York

Sandy Gade
Project Editor
LearningExpress
New York, New York

Melinda Grove
Adjunct Professor
Quinnipiac University and Naugatuck Valley Community College
Math Consultant

Karen Hunter
Project Editor
Elkview, West Virginia

Diane Kampf
Middle School English Teacher, Grade 7
Robert Moss Middle School
North Babylon School District
North Babylon, New York
Adjunct Assistant Professor
Suffolk Community College
Suffolk, New York

Noah Kravitz
Curriculum and Technology Specialist
New York, New York

Kerry McLean
Project Editor
Math Tutor
Shirley, New York

Kimberly Moroz
English Instructor
Wilmington College
New Castle, Delaware

William Recco
Middle School Math Teacher, Grade 8
New York Shoreham/Wading River School District
Math Tutor
St. James, New York

Colleen Schultz
Middle School Math Teacher, Grade 8
Vestal Central School District
Math Tutor and Teacher Mentor
Vestal, New York

Contents

Introduction

Welcome to *501 Sentence Completion Questions!* This book is designed to help you prepare for the verbal and reading sections of many assessment and entrance exams. By completing the 501 sample items offered here and by studying their answer explanations, you will develop the skills necessary to tackle each type of sentence completion question. You will also improve your vocabulary and your process of elimination skills.

Sentence completions test your ability to use the information found in complex, but incomplete, sentences in order to correctly complete the sentences. Sentence completions test two separate aspects of your verbal skills: your vocabulary and your ability to follow the internal logic of sentences. These sentences are often quite complex. Fortunately, there are some strategies that will greatly increase your score on these questions. Each of these questions has one blank (or, on some tests, two blanks) within a single sentence. Often the sentences are long and difficult to follow, but with practice you can learn to master them.

Many standardized tests—including high school and college entrance exams and civil service exams—use sentence completion questions to test vocabulary and logic. Some of the "alphabet soup" of exams that contain sentence completions are the:

- SAT I exam
- PSAT/NMSQT exam
- GRE General test
- TOEFL/TOEIC exams
- ISEE
- GRT

You might wonder what kinds of strategies you can use to master sentence completions. When it comes to sentence completions, the word that does *not* appear is the key to the meaning of the sentence. The words that *do* appear offer *clues* to the missing word. If you can find out how the words that appear are connected, you can find the correct answer. This means that you must know more than just the meaning of the words involved. You must also understand the logic of the sentence. Here is a sampling of strategies:

- Read the entire sentence saying "blank" for the blank(s). This gives you an overall sense of the meaning of the sentence and helps you figure out how the parts of the sentence relate to each other. If an answer occurs to you before you even look at the choices, you may have a synonym for the answer or the answer itself.
- Pay special attention to introductory and transitional words—*but, although, however, yet, even though*—because they are key to forming the logical structure of the sentence.
- Be sure your choice is both logical and grammatically correct.
- If you don't know some words, use elimination and educated guessing, which means you are able to eliminate

one or more of the choices as definitely wrong; or guessing from context when you know a related word.

There are several types of sentence completions:

- restatement
- comparison
- contrast
- cause and effect

Here is an example of a cause-and-effect sentence completion question:

After a brief and violent _____ that ousted the president, General Monsanto declared himself the dictator of the country.

a. nuance
b. coup
c. solicitation
d. upbraiding
e. lament

The answer is choice **b**. A *coup* (n.) is a sudden and decisive change of leadership illegally or by force, a takeover. What (the cause) led the general to declare himself dictator (the result)? Something *brief and violent, that ousted the president*, a coup.

Here is an example of a restatement question:

The city council formed a committee to simplify several dozen _____ city ordinances that were unnecessarily complicated and out-of-date.

a. feckless
b. empirical
c. byzantine
d. slovenly
e. pedantic

The answer is choice **c**, *byzantine*, an adjective that means "highly complicated and intricate." Here, you are looking for a restatement of the clue words *complicated* and *out-of-date*, and for something that needs *simplifying*.

As you practice sentence completions, you may discover *signal* words and phrases—clues that help you choose the correct answer. Here are common signal words and an example for each kind of question:

Restatement: *namely, in other words, in fact, that is*
Example: The pickpocket was a trickster, *in other words*, a _____.
(The answer, which restates "trickster," might be *knave* or *scoundrel.*)

Comparison: *likewise, similarly, and, just as, as* _____ *as, for example, as shown, as illustrated by*
Example: Anna was cleared of all charges; *similarly*, Sam was

_____.

(The answer compares to being "cleared of all charges," so perhaps Sam was *vindicated.*)

Contrast: *though, although, however, despite, but, yet; on the other hand, but, however, despite,* or *on the contrary*
Example: *Although* the tiger is a solitary beast, its cousin the lion is a _____ animal.
(The answer is something that contrasts with "solitary," such as *gregarious* or *sociable.*)

Cause and effect: *thus, therefore, consequently,* and *because* and phrases such as *due to, as a result, leads to*
Example: A truck stole her parking spot; *consequently*, Sally's _____ look showed her displeasure.
(The answer would be a look caused by someone stealing Sally's parking spot, maybe *scowling* or *sullen.*)

The sentence completion question sets in this book increase in difficulty as you practice your way through them—from easy to intermediate to advanced. These divisions may reflect how challenging the vocabulary is or how complex the sentence structure is or how challenging the logic of the sentence is.

The 501 Skill Builder in Focus exercises will help you prepare for an exam in several ways. First, you will become familiar with the question format. You will get used to identifying the relationships of words within a sentence. The more comfortable you are with the question format and the more familiar you are with the range of sentence completion types, the easier the verbal or reading section of your test will be.

Second, your performance on these questions will help you assess your vocabulary strengths and weaknesses. For example, you may find that you do very well with words that are cognates (words from a common original form, such as *asteroid* and *astronomy*), but not so well on foreign words, such as *ennui* or *angst*.

Third, you will learn, through practice, to spot and disregard wrong answer choices. You may also discover a pattern to your wrong answers. (Are you weak on cause-and-effect questions?)

In addition to this book, look for other sources of vocabulary growth: software, audio and online courses, and books. One helpful resource is LearningExpress's *Vocabulary and Spelling Success in 20 Minutes a Day*, which helps boost your vocabulary and your verbal test scores.

You have already taken an important step toward improving your score. You have shown your commitment by purchasing this book. Now what you need to do is complete each exercise, study the answers, and watch your ability to solve sentence completions increase. Good luck!

Chapter 1

1. She hadn't eaten all day, and by the time she got home she was
    _____.
    a. blighted
    b. confutative
    c. ravenous
    d. ostentatious
    e. blissful

2. The movie offended many of the parents of its younger viewers by
    including unnecessary _____ in the dialogue.
    a. vulgarity
    b. verbosity
    c. vocalizations
    d. garishness
    e. tonality

3. His neighbors found his _____ manner bossy and irritating, and
they stopped inviting him to backyard barbeques.
   a. insentient
   b. magisterial
   c. reparatory
   d. restorative
   e. modest

4. Steven is always _____ about showing up for work because he
feels that tardiness is a sign of irresponsibility.
   a. legible
   b. tolerable
   c. punctual
   d. literal
   e. belligerent

5. Candace would _____ her little sister into an argument by teasing
her and calling her names.
   a. advocate
   b. provoke
   c. perforate
   d. lamente
   e. expunge

6. The dress Ariel wore _____ with small, glassy beads, creating a
shimmering effect.
   a. titillated
   b. reiterated
   c. scintillated
   d. enthralled
   e. striated

7. Being able to afford this luxury car will _____ getting a better-
paying job.
   a. maximize
   b. recombinant
   c. reiterate
   d. necessitate
   e. reciprocate

8. Levina unknowingly _____ the thief by holding open the elevator doors and ensuring his escape.

   a. coerced

   b. proclaimed

   c. abetted

   d. sanctioned

   e. solicited

9. Shakespeare, a(n) _____ writer, entertained audiences by writing many tragic and comic plays.

   a. numeric

   b. obstinate

   c. dutiful

   d. prolific

   e. generic

10. I had the _____ experience of sitting next to an over-talkative passenger on my flight home from Brussels.

   a. satisfactory

   b. commendable

   c. galling

   d. acceptable

   e. acute

11. Prince Phillip had to choose: marry the woman he loved and _____ his right to the throne, or marry Lady Fiona and inherit the crown.

   a. reprimand

   b. upbraid

   c. abdicate

   d. winnow

   e. extol

12. If you will not do your work of your own _____, I have no choice but to penalize you if it is not done on time.

   a. predilection

   b. coercion

   c. excursion

   d. volition

   e. infusion

13. After sitting in the sink for several days, the dirty, food-encrusted dishes became _____.
a. malodorous
b. prevalent
c. imposing
d. perforated
e. emphatic

14. Giulia soon discovered the source of the _____ smell in the room: a week-old tuna sandwich that one of the children had hidden in the closet.
a. quaint
b. fastidious
c. clandestine
d. laconic
e. fetid

15. After making _____ remarks to the President, the reporter was not invited to return to the White House pressroom.
a. hospitable
b. itinerant
c. enterprising
d. chivalrous
e. irreverent

16. With her _____ eyesight, Krystyna spotted a trio of deer on the hillside and she reduced the speed of her car.
a. inferior
b. keen
c. impressionable
d. ductile
e. conspiratorial

17. With a(n) _____ grin, the boy quickly slipped the candy into his pocket without his mother's knowledge.
a. jaundiced
b. nefarious
c. stereotypical
d. sentimental
e. impartial

18. Her _____ display of tears at work did not impress her new boss, who felt she should try to control her emotions.
a. maudlin
b. meritorious
c. precarious
d. plausible
e. schematic

19. Johan argued, "If you know about a crime but don't report it, you are _____ in that crime because you allowed it to happen."
a. acquitted
b. steadfast
c. tenuous
d. complicit
e. nullified

20. The authorities, fearing a _____ of their power, called for a military state in the hopes of restoring order.
a. subversion
b. premonition
c. predilection
d. infusion
e. inversion

21. The story's bitter antagonist felt such great _____ for all of the other characters that as a result, his life was very lonely and he died alone.
a. insurgence
b. malevolence
c. reciprocation
d. declamation
e. preference

22. It is difficult to believe that charging 20% on an outstanding credit card balance isn't _____!
   a. bankruptcy
   b. usury
   c. novice
   d. kleptomania
   e. flagrancy

23. The _____ weather patterns of the tropical island meant tourists had to carry both umbrellas and sunglasses.
   a. impertinent
   b. supplicant
   c. preeminent
   d. illustrative
   e. kaleidoscopic

24. Wedding ceremonies often include the exchange of _____ rings to symbolize the couple's promises to each other.
   a. hirsute
   b. acrimonious
   c. plaintive
   d. deciduous
   e. votive

25. Kym was _____ in choosing her friends, so her parties were attended by vastly different and sometimes bizarre personalities.
   a. indispensable
   b. indiscriminate
   c. commensurate
   d. propulsive
   e. indisputable

Answers

1. **c.** *Ravenous* (adj.) means extremely hungry.

2. **a.** *Vulgarity* (n.) means offensive speech or conduct.

3. **b.** *Magisterial* (adj.) means overbearing or offensively self-assured.

4. **c.** *Punctual* (adj.) means arriving exactly on time.

5. **b.** To *provoke* (v.) is to incite anger or resentment; to call forth a feeling or action.

6. **c.** To *scintillate* (v.) means to emit or send forth sparks or little flashes of light, creating a shimmering effect; to sparkle.

7. **d.** To *necessitate* (v.) means to make necessary, especially as a result.

8. **c.** To *abet* (v.) means to assist, encourage, urge, or aid, usually an act of wrongdoing.

9. **d.** *Prolific* (adj.) means abundantly creative.

10. **c.** *Galling* (adj.) means irritating, annoying, or exasperating.

11. **c.** To *abdicate* (v.) means to formally relinquish or surrender power, office, or responsibility.

12. **d.** *Volition* (n.) means accord; an act or exercise of will.

13. **a.** *Malodorous* (adj.) means having a foul-smelling odor.

14. **e.** *Fetid* (adj.) means having a foul or offensive odor, putrid.

15. **e.** *Irreverent* (adj.) means lacking respect or seriousness; not reverent.

16. **b.** *Keen* (adj.) means being extremely sensitive or responsive; having strength of perception.

17. **b.** *Nefarious* (adj.) means wicked, vicious, or evil.

18. **a.** *Maudlin* (adj.) means excessively and weakly sentimental or tearfully emotional.

19. **d.** *Complicit* (adj.) means participating in or associated with a questionable act or a crime.

20. **a.** *Subversion* (n.) means an overthrow, as from the foundation.

21. **b.** *Malevolence* (n.) means ill will or malice toward others; hate.

22. **b.** *Usury* (n.) is the lending of money at exorbitant interest rates.

23. **e.** *Kaleidoscopic* (adj.) means continually changing or quickly shifting.

24. **e.** *Votive* (adj.) means dedicated by a vow.

25. **b.** *Indiscriminate* (adj.) means not discriminating or choosing randomly; haphazard; without distinction.

Chapter 2

26. Phillip's _____ tone endeared him to his comical friends, but irritated his serious father.
    a. aloof
    b. jesting
    c. grave
    d. earnest
    e. conservative

27. Brian's pale Irish skin was _____ to burn if he spent too much time in the sun.
    a. prone
    b. urbane
    c. eminent
    d. erect
    e. daunted

28. A fan of historical fiction, Joline is now reading a novel about slavery in the _____ South.
a. decorous
b. rogue
c. droll
d. antebellum
e. onerous

29. Over the years the Wilsons slowly _____ upon the Jacksons' property, moving the stone markers that divided their lots farther and farther onto the Jacksons' land.
a. encroached
b. jettisoned
c. conjoined
d. repudiated
e. teemed

30. Mary became _____ at typing because she practiced every day for six months.
a. proficient
b. reflective
c. dormant
d. redundant
e. valiant

31. To find out what her husband bought for her birthday, Susan attempted to _____ his family members about his recent shopping excursions.
a. prescribe
b. probe
c. alienate
d. converge
e. revere

32. Juan's friends found him in a _____ mood after he learned he would be homecoming king.
   a. jovial
   b. stealthy
   c. paltry
   d. gullible
   e. depleted

33. His suit of armor made the knight _____ to his enemy's attack, and he was able to escape safely to his castle.
   a. vulnerable
   b. churlish
   c. invulnerable
   d. static
   e. imprudent

34. Choosing a small, fuel-efficient car is a _____ purchase for a recent college graduate.
   a. corrupt
   b. tedious
   c. unhallowed
   d. sardonic
   e. judicious

35. Such a _____ violation of school policy should be punished by nothing less than expulsion.
   a. copious
   b. flagrant
   c. raucous
   d. nominal
   e. morose

36. With all of the recent negative events in her life, she felt _____ forces must be at work.
   a. resurgent
   b. premature
   c. malignant
   d. punctilious
   e. antecedent

37. The _____ rumors did a great deal of damage even though they turned out to be false.
    a. bemused
    b. prosaic
    c. apocryphal
    d. ebullient
    e. tantamount

38. When her schoolwork got to be too much, Pam had a tendency to _____, which always put her further behind.
    a. dedicate
    b. rejuvenate
    c. ponder
    d. excel
    e. procrastinate

39. Racha's glance was a _____ invitation to speak later in private about events of the meeting.
    a. trecherous
    b. scintillating
    c. tactful
    d. tacit
    e. taboo

40. She reached the _____ of her career with her fourth novel, which won the Pulitzer Prize.
    a. harbinger
    b. apogee
    c. metamorphosis
    d. dictum
    e. synthesis

41. The _____ townspeople celebrated the soldier's return to his home by adorning trees with yellow ribbons and balloons.
    a. somber
    b. jubilant
    c. pitiless
    d. cunning
    e. unsullied

42. The governor-elect was hounded by a group of _____ lobbyists and others hoping to gain favor with her administration.
   a. facetious
   b. abstruse
   c. magnanimous
   d. fawning
   e. saccharine

43. The mock graduation ceremony—with a trained skunk posing as the college president—was a complete _____ that offended many college officials.
   a. tempest
   b. epitome
   c. quintessence
   d. travesty
   e. recitative

44. The busy, _____ fabric of the clown's tie matched his oversized jacket, which was equally atrocious.
   a. mottled
   b. bleak
   c. credible
   d. malleable
   e. communicable

45. Kendrick's talent _____ under the tutelage of Anya Kowalonek, who as a young woman had been the most accomplished pianist in her native Lithuania.
   a. bantered
   b. touted
   c. flourished
   d. embellished
   e. colluded

46. The children were _____ by the seemingly nonsensical clues until Kinan pointed out that the messages were in code.
   a. censured
   b. striated
   c. feigned
   d. prevaricated
   e. flummoxed

47. As the _____ in Romeo and Juliet, Romeo is a hero able to capture the audience's sympathy by continually professing his love for Juliet.
   a. protagonist
   b. enigma
   c. facade
   d. activist
   e. catechist

48. The chess master promised to _____ havoc upon his opponent's pawns for taking his bishop.
   a. wreak
   b. warrant
   c. ensue
   d. placate
   e. endow

49. I have always admired Seymour's _____; I've never seen him rattled by anything.
   a. aplomb
   b. confluence
   c. propriety
   d. compunction
   e. nostalgia

50. The soldiers received a military _____ to inspect all their vehicles before traveling.
   a. allotment
   b. dominion
   c. affectation
   d. calculation
   e. mandate

Answers

26.   **b.**   *Jesting* (adj.) means characterized by making jests; joking; playful.

27.   **a.**   *Prone* (adj.) means a tendency or inclination to something.

28.   **d.**   *Antebellum* (adj.) means belonging to the period before a war, especially the American Civil War.

29.   **a.**   To *encroach* (v.) means to gradually or stealthily take the rights or possessions of another; to advance beyond proper or formal limits; trespass.

30.   **a.**   *Proficient* (adj.) means well versed in any business or branch of learning; adept.

31.   **b.**   To *probe* (v.) is to examine thoroughly; tentatively survey.

32.   **a.**   *Jovial* (adj.) means showing hearty good cheer; marked with the spirit of jolly merriment.

33.   **c.**   *Invulnerable* (adj.) means incapable of being damaged or wounded; unassailable or invincible.

34.   **e.**   *Judicious* (adj.) means being wise or prudent; showing good judgment; sensible.

35.   **b.**   *Flagrant* (adj.) means conspicuously and outrageously bad, offensive, or reprehensible.

36.   **c.**   *Malignant* (adj.) means disposed to cause distress or inflict suffering intentionally; inclining to produce death; an injurious infiltration.

37.   **c.**   *Apocryphal* (adj.) means of questionable authenticity or doubtful authority; fictitious, false.

38.   **e.**   To *procrastinate* (v.) is to put off from day to day.

39. **c.** *Tacit* (adj.) means unspoken yet understood.

40. **b.** *Apogee* (n.) means the highest or farthest point, culmination; the point in its orbit where a satellite is at the greatest distance from the body it is orbiting.

41. **b.** *Jubilant* (adj.) means rejoicing; expressing joyfulness; exulting.

42. **d.** *Fawning* (adj.) means attempting to win favor or attention by excessive flattery, ingratiating displays of affection, or servile compliance; obsequious.

43. **d.** *Travesty* (n.) means a parody; a grotesque imitation with the intent to ridicule.

44. **a.** *Mottled* (adj.) means blotched or spotted with different colors or shades.

45. **c.** To *flourish* (v.) is (of artists) to be in a state of high productivity, excellence, or influence; to grow luxuriously, thrive; to fare well, prosper, increase in wealth, honor, comfort or whatever is desirable; to make bold, sweeping movements.

46. **e.** To *flummox* (v.) is to confuse, perplex, bewilder.

47. **a.** A *protagonist* (n.) is the main character in a drama.

48. **a.** To *wreak* (v.) means to inflict, as a revenge or punishment.

49. **a.** *Aplomb* (n.) is self-assurance, composure, poise, especially under strain.

50. **e.** *Mandate* (n.) is a command or authoritative instruction.

Chapter 3

51. As _____ beings we live each day conscious of our shortcomings and victories.
  a. sensational
  b. sentient
  c. sentimental
  d. static
  e. senile

52. The curious crowd gathered to watch the irate customer _____ about the poor service he received in the restaurant.
  a. antiquate
  b. trivialize
  c. rant
  d. placate
  e. fetter

53. The man's _____ driving resulted in a four-car pile-up on the freeway.
a. burdensome
b. charismatic
c. exceptional
d. boastful
e. negligent

54. Ron didn't know the rules of rugby, but he could tell by the crowd's reaction that it was a critical _____ in the game.
a. acclamation
b. conviction
c. juncture
d. enigma
e. revelation

55. My ancestor who lost his life in the Revolutionary War was a _____ for American independence.
a. knave
b. reactionary
c. compatriot
d. nonconformist
e. martyr

56. The _____ sound of the radiator as it released steam became an increasingly annoying distraction.
a. sibilant
b. scintillating
c. diverting
d. sinuous
e. scurrilous

57. It is helpful for salesmen to develop a good _____ with their customers in order to gain their trust.
a. platitude
b. rapport
c. ire
d. tribute
e. disinclination

58. In such a small office setting, the office manager found he had
_____ responsibilities that required knowledge in a variety of
different topics.
a. heedless
b. complementary
c. mutual
d. manifold
e. correlative

59. David's _____ entrance on stage disrupted the scene and caused
the actors to flub their lines.
a. untimely
b. precise
c. lithe
d. fortuitous
e. tensile

60. The settlers found an ideal location with plenty of _____ land for
farming and a mountain stream for fresh water and irrigation.
a. candid
b. provincial
c. arable
d. timid
e. quaint

61. The _____ seventh-grader towered over the other players on his
basketball team.
a. gangling
b. studious
c. mimetic
d. abject
e. reserved

62. Carson was at first flattered by the _____ of his new colleagues, but he soon realized that their admiration rested chiefly on his connections, not his accomplishments.
a. reprisal
b. adulation
c. bulwark
d. rapport
e. retinue

63. For a(n) _____ fee, it is possible to upgrade from regular gasoline to premium.
a. nominal
b. judgmental
c. existential
d. bountiful
e. jovial

64. Searching frantically to find the hidden jewels, the thieves proceeded to _____ the entire house.
a. justify
b. darken
c. amplify
d. ransack
e. glorify

65. The _____ deer stuck close to its mother when venturing out into the open field.
a. starling
b. foundling
c. yearling
d. begrudging
e. hatchling

66. The police officer _____ the crowd to step back from the fire so
that no one would get hurt.
a. undulated
b. enjoined
c. stagnated
d. permeated
e. delineated

67. Jackson's poor typing skills were a _____ to finding employment
at the nearby office complex.
a. benefit
b. hindrance
c. partiality
d. temptation
e. canon

68. Through _____, the chef created a creamy sauce by combining
brown sugar, butter, and cinnamon in a pan and cooking them over
medium-high heat.
a. impasse
b. obscurity
c. decadence
d. diversion
e. liquefaction

69. The defendant claimed that he was innocent and that his
confession was _____.
a. coerced
b. flagrant
c. terse
d. benign
e. futile

70. Harvey was discouraged that his visa application was _____ due to his six convictions.
   a. lethargic
   b. immeasurable
   c. nullified
   d. segregated
   e. aggravated

71. The rebel spies were charged with _____ and put on trial.
   a. sedition
   b. attrition
   c. interaction
   d. reiteration
   e. perdition

72. Keith was _____ in his giving to friends and charities throughout the year, not just during the holidays.
   a. munificent
   b. portly
   c. amphibious
   d. guileful
   e. forensic

73. Calvin reached the _____ of his career in his early thirties when he became president and CEO of a software company.
   a. zephyr
   b. plethora
   c. vale
   d. nocturne
   e. zenith

74. Although I'd asked a simple "yes" or "no" question, Irfan's reply was _____, and I didn't know how to interpret it.
   a. prodigal
   b. irate
   c. equivocal
   d. voracious
   e. harrowing

75. The high-profile company CEO was given an _____ for speaking
at the monthly meeting of the area business leaders' society.

    a. expiation

    b. honorarium

    c. inoculation

    d. interpretation

    e. inquisition

Answers

51. **b.** *Sentient* (adj.) means possessing the power of sense or sense-perception; conscious.

52. **c.** To *rant* (v.) means to speak loudly or violently.

53. **e.** *Negligent* (adj.) means to habitually lack in giving proper care or attention; having a careless manner.

54. **c.** *Juncture* (n.) is a point of time, especially one that is at a critical point.

55. **e.** A *martyr* (n.) is one who sacrifices something of supreme value, such as a life, for a cause or principle; a victim; one who suffers constantly.

56. **a.** *Sibilant* (adj.) means characterized by a hissing sound.

57. **b.** A *rapport* (n.) is a relationship that is useful and harmonious.

58. **d.** *Manifold* (adj.) means many and varied; of many kinds; multiple.

59. **a.** *Untimely* (adj.) means happening before the proper time.

60. **c.** *Arable* (adj.) means suitable for cultivation, fit for plowing and farming productively.

61. **a.** *Gangling* (adj.) means awkward, lanky, or unusually tall and thin.

62. **b.** *Adulation* (n.) means strong or excessive admiration or praise; fawning flattery.

63. **a.** *Nominal* (adj.) means small, virtually nothing, or much below the actual value of a thing.

64. **d.** To *ransack* (v.) means to thoroughly search, to plunder, pillage.

65. **c.** A *yearling* (n.) is a young animal past its first year but not yet two years old.

66. **b.** To *enjoin* (v.) means to issue an order or command; to direct or impose with authority.

67. **b.** *Hindrance* (n.) is an impediment or obstruction; a state of being hindered; a cause of being prevented or impeded.

68. **e.** *Liquefaction* (n.) is the process of liquefying a solid or making a liquid.

69. **a.** To *coerce* (v.) is to force to do through pressure, threats, or intimidation; to compel.

70. **c.** To *nullify* (v.) means to make invalid or nonexistent.

71. **a.** *Sedition* (n.) means resistance, insurrection; conduct directed against public order and the tranquility of the state.

72. **a.** *Munificent* (adj.) means extremely generous or liberal in giving; lavish.

73. **e.** *Zenith* (n.) means the highest point of any path or course.

74. **c.** *Equivocal* (adj.) means open to two or more interpretations, ambiguous and often intended to mislead; open to question, uncertain.

75. **b.** *Honorarium* (n.) is payment or reward for services for which payment is not usually required.

Chapter 4

76. Zachary was doomed to a miserable life, for no matter how much he had, he always _____ the possessions of others.
   a. protracted
   b. exalted
   c. engendered
   d. coveted
   e. filibustered

77. Sheila's grueling hike included passing through numerous _____.
   a. terrariums
   b. neoprene
   c. jurisdictions
   d. ravines
   e. belfries

78. The college professor was known on campus as a _____ character—bland but harmless and noble in his ideals.
  a. staid
  b. stagnant
  c. auspicious
  d. sterile
  e. dogmatic

79. Because he was so _____, the athlete was able to complete the obstacle course in record time.
  a. belligerent
  b. nimble
  c. demure
  d. volatile
  e. speculative

80. The toy store's extensive inventory offered a _____ of toys from baby items to video games for teenagers.
  a. manifold
  b. lexicon
  c. burrow
  d. gamut
  e. motif

81. With sunscreen and a good book, April _____ by the pool in her lounge chair while the children swam.
  a. ensconced
  b. sustained
  c. expelled
  d. transcended
  e. lolled

82. NaQuan had a terrible habit of boasting so much about his smallest accomplishments that his _____ became renowned throughout the small college campus.
   a. vainglory
   b. timidity
   c. diffidence
   d. tempestuousness
   e. mockery

83. Only a small number of people in the audience laughed at the comic's _____ sense of humor, while the rest found him to be too sarcastic.
   a. consequential
   b. avaricious
   c. venturous
   d. dauntless
   e. mordant

84. He has long been a(n) _____ of year-round school, believing it would significantly improve learning and ease the burden on working parents.
   a. advocate
   b. levity
   c. detractor
   d. epiphany
   e. connoisseur

85. Tired of hearing the child whine for more candy, the babysitter finally _____ and offered him a piece of chocolate.
   a. relented
   b. abated
   c. rendered
   d. placated
   e. enumerated

86. Dogs growl and show their teeth in an attempt to _____ the animal or person they perceive as a threat.
   a. bolster
   b. waylay
   c. cow
   d. exacerbate
   e. appease

87. In biology class, Sabine observed the slug's _____, its barely discernible movement in the tank.
   a. parody
   b. prescience
   c. torpor
   d. insight
   e. vigor

88. The _____ instinct of a watchdog is to attack strangers who enter its home.
   a. judicious
   b. intimate
   c. pragmatic
   d. melancholy
   e. primal

89. The battalion's _____ was a well-fortified structure near the enemy lines.
   a. labyrinth
   b. summary
   c. villa
   d. vinculum
   e. garrison

90. Much to my surprise, my teenage daughter was _____ to the idea of going out with me on Friday night instead of with her friends.
   a. contrite
   b. impartial
   c. partisan
   d. deferential
   e. amenable

91. The enormous waves forced the lobster boat to _____ heavily to the starboard side, causing crates of lobsters to topple and fall into the ocean.
   a. trifle
   b. degenerate
   c. list
   d. expedite
   e. disseminate

92. Walking through the _____ forest in spring was a welcome escape from the cold, gray winter we had spent in the city.
   a. pliant
   b. verdant
   c. factious
   d. bland
   e. innocuous

93. Nina called the humane society when she saw her neighbor _____ his dog.
   a. mandate
   b. forebode
   c. maltreat
   d. stipulate
   e. peruse

94. Meredith used the _____ to steer the horse and keep him in line.
   a. jolt
   b. bristle
   c. chine
   d. quirt
   e. hearth

95. Oliver was unable to _____ himself from the difficulties he had caused by forging the documents.
   a. reprove
   b. pique
   c. oust
   d. extricate
   e. broach

96. The _____ of our expedition was still so far away that I felt we would never get there.
a. nadir
b. terminus
c. speculation
d. apex
e. dungeon

97. If he expected to _____ as a doctor, Lou knew he would have to study hard in medical school and work long hours to gain experience and skill.
a. perpetrate
b. palliate
c. palpitate
d. prosper
e. mediate

98. Doc Wilson grew up in Florida and was not prepared to face the _____ climate of the Alaskan winter.
a. freshwater
b. gelid
c. compendious
d. subsidiary
e. improvident

99. Marvin's _____ prevented him from finishing his work and was evidenced in his large phone bills.
a. loquacity
b. heroism
c. decadence
d. depreciation
e. rescission

100. The graph clearly showed the company reaching the _____ in profits during the 1980s when the economy was in a boom period.

    a. narthex

    b. gullet

    c. gamut

    d. quiescence

    e. vertex

Answers

76. d. To *covet* (v.) is to wish or long for; to feel immoderate desire for that which belongs to another.

77. d. A *ravine* (n.) is a deep narrow canyon.

78. a. *Staid* (adj.) means of a steady and sober character; prudently reserved and colorless.

79. b. *Nimble* (adj.) is quick and light in movement, to be agile.

80. d. A *gamut* (n.) is an entire range or a whole series.

81. e. To *loll* (v.) is to lean, recline, or act lazily or indolently; lounge.

82. a. *Vainglory* (n.) means excessive, pretentious, and demonstrative vanity.

83. e. *Mordant* (adj.) means bitingly sarcastic or harshly caustic.

84. a. An *advocate* (n.) is one who argues for a cause, a supporter or defender; one who pleads on another's behalf.

85. a. To *relent* (v.) means to yield or comply.

86. c. To *cow* (v.) is to intimidate, frighten with threats or show of force.

87. c. *Torpor* (n.) means extreme sluggishness; lethargy or apathy; dullness.

88. e. *Primal* (adj.) means primary, the first in order or the original; primitive.

89. e. A *garrison* (n.) is a fort or outpost where troops are stationed; any military post.

90. **e.** *Amenable* (adj.) means disposed or willing to comply; responsive, willing; responsible to a higher authority, accountable.

91. **c.** To *list* (v.) (related to a vessel) is to incline or to cause to lean to one side.

92. **b.** *Verdant* (adj.) means green with vegetation.

93. **c.** To *maltreat* (v.) means to treat poorly; abuse.

94. **d.** A *quirt* (n.) is a riding whip with a short handle and braided rawhide leash.

95. **d.** To *extricate* (v.) is to release from an entanglement or difficulty, disengage.

96. **b.** The *terminus* (n) is the final point or goal; the final stop on a transportation line.

97. **d.** To *prosper* (v.) means to be successful.

98. **b.** *Gelid* (adj.) means icy or extremely cold; possessing a cold or unfriendly manner.

99. **a.** *Loquacity* (n.) is talkativeness; the state of continual talking.

100. **e.** *Vertex* (n.) means the highest point of anything; the apex or summit.

Chapter 5

101. Amie agrees with the _____ that the grass is always greener on the other side of the fence.
    a. perpetuity
    b. penchant
    c. maxim
    d. conformation
    e. fortitude

102. Victor Frankenstein's creature was a(n) _____, detested by everyone he met.
    a. itinerant
    b. anathema
    c. cosmopolitan
    d. mercenary
    e. anomaly

103. Jack Nicholson was at the _____ of his career when he received the Oscar for Best Actor.

    a. detriment
    b. pinnacle
    c. oligarchy
    d. rogue
    e. repose

104. Ariana was outstanding as the moderator; she handled the intensely heated debate with great _____, diplomatically and tactfully keeping the conversation fair and on track.

    a. finesse
    b. pretentiousness
    c. prowess
    d. succor
    e. aversion

105. The class endured a loud and lengthy _____ by the teacher on the subject of submitting written work on time.

    a. guile
    b. polemic
    c. bravado
    d. tirade
    e. heresy

106. Lauren's _____ features, what you first noticed about her, were her stunning black hair and large, dark eyes.

    a. savvy
    b. affluent
    c. predominant
    d. universal
    e. malicious

107. Whenever Tom and I would argue he would _____ with his hands and body to accentuate his point.
a. interject
b. infuse
c. gesticulate
d. conjure
e. encumber

108. Must we be subjected to your _____ complaints all day long?
a. tiresome
b. fearsome
c. awesome
d. gleesome
e. wholesome

109. The new political candidate refused to print _____ about her aggressive opponent, but that did not stop him from printing lies about her.
a. dispensation
b. assignation
c. rendition
d. libel
e. compunction

110. Awkwardly tall and prone to tripping over her own feet, Grace felt her name was truly a _____.
a. misnomer
b. preoccupation
c. universality
d. garrulity
e. benevolence

111. Although the villagers' lives were profoundly different from her own, Jing-Mae felt a deep _____ for the people when she served in the Peace Corps.
a. reparation
b. affinity
c. injunction
d. exigency
e. analogy

112. Sometimes late at night Sharon would gaze joyfully at her children as they slept and _____ in their innocence.
a. sneer
b. ostracize
c. revel
d. repudiate
e. antiquate

113. In the famous balcony scene, Romeo _____ Juliet's beauty in one of the most romantic soliloquies ever written.
a. sanctions
b. extols
c. peruses
d. beguiles
e. fetters

114. It was _____ to think that it could possibly snow in the middle of the desert.
a. advantageous
b. philosophical
c. eroding
d. preventative
e. preposterous

115. Every evening at the restaurant, the reporter would eavesdrop on the Mayor's conversations in order to _____ any information that could make headlines.

   a. ignore
   b. glean
   c. extol
   d. extend
   e. narrate

116. The surgeon placed a _____ on the femoral artery to bind it during the long and exhausting surgery.

   a. ligature
   b. doctrine
   c. premise
   d. synopsis
   e. degeneration

117. By sheer _____ force, the men pushed the truck to the side of the road and out of danger.

   a. virile
   b. persnickety
   c. meticulous
   d. suave
   e. contentious

118. Based on his recent poor decisions, it was obvious that Seth lacked even a _____ of good sense.

   a. debasement
   b. diversion
   c. disapprobation
   d. submission
   e. modicum

119. To settle the dispute, the students elected a faculty member to serve as a(n) _____.
   a. maverick
   b. dystopia
   c. arbiter
   d. fiduciary
   e. martyr

120. The _____ newspaper accounts of the city scandal caused some readers to question the truth of the stories.
   a. lurid
   b. vivacious
   c. blithesome
   d. prolific
   e. amicable

121. The _____ man with amnesia was unable to recognize where he was.
   a. endogenous
   b. euphoric
   c. nonplussed
   d. amicable
   e. pliable

122. Justin's _____ solution to the problem revealed that he did not spend much time considering the consequences.
   a. facile
   b. obsolete
   c. resilient
   d. pristine
   e. ardent

123. The events of the evening _____ without difficulty despite the lack of planning on the part of the host.
   a. expired
   b. transpired
   c. retired
   d. ensured
   e. extorted

124. It is every American person's _____ to live the life he or she chooses.
   a. composite
   b. eloquence
   c. prerogative
   d. allusion
   e. demise

125. After the boisterous customers left the café without tipping, Carlos _____ at them through the restaurant's front window.
   a. interjected
   b. jostled
   c. glowered
   d. emulated
   e. skulked

Answers

101. **c.** *Maxim* (n.) is an established principle or a general truth, often a condensed version of a practical truth.

102. **b.** An *anathema* (n.) is one who is detested or shunned; one who is cursed or damned; a curse or vehement denunciation; a formal ban, curse, or excommunication.

103. **b.** A *pinnacle* (n.) is the highest level or degree available.

104. **a.** *Finesse* (n.) is the subtle, skillful handling of a situation, diplomacy, tact; refined or delicate performance or execution.

105. **d.** A *tirade* (n.) is a long and blusterous speech given especially when the speaker is denouncing someone or something.

106. **c.** *Predominant* (adj.) means most dominant, common, or frequent; to have surpassing power, influence, or authority.

107. **c.** To *gesticulate* (v.) means to use gestures or make motions; express through motion, especially while speaking.

108. **a.** *Tiresome* (adj.) means causing to be weary.

109. **d.** *Libel* (n.) is defamatory writing; misrepresentative publication (writing, pictures, signs) that damages a person's reputation.

110. **a.** *Misnomer* (n.) is a misnaming of a person or place; a wrong or unsuitable name.

111. **b.** An *affinity* (n.) is a natural attraction or liking; a feeling of kinship, connection or closeness, similarity; relationship by marriage.

112. **c.** To *revel* (v.) is to take great pleasure or delight.

113. **b.** To *extol* (v.) means to praise highly, exalt, glorify.

114. **e.** *Preposterous* (adj.) means contrary to common sense or utterly absurd.

115. **b.** To *glean* (v.) means to gather or collect slowly; to learn or discover bit by bit.

116. **a.** A *ligature* (n.) is something that ties or binds up, such as a bandage, wire, or cord.

117. **a.** *Virile* (adj.) means having masculine strength; vigorous or energetic.

118. **e.** *Modicum* (n.) is a small or token amount.

119. **c.** An *arbiter* (n.) is one selected or appointed to judge or decide a disputed issue, an arbitrator; someone with the power to settle matters at will.

120. **a.** *Lurid* (adj.) means glaringly sensational or vivid; shocking.

121. **c.** *Nonplussed* (adj.) means greatly perplexed, filled with bewilderment.

122. **a.** *Facile* (adj.) means arrived at or achieved with little difficulty or effort, thus lacking depth, superficial; performing or speaking effectively with effortless ease and fluency, adroit, eloquent.

123. **b.** To *transpire* (v.) means to come to pass, to occur.

124. **c.** *Prerogative* (n.) means an exclusive or special right or privilege.

125. **c.** To *glower* (v.) means to stare angrily or sullenly, to look intently with anger or dislike.

Chapter 6

126. People often referred to Noelle as _____ because she trusted everyone and even slept with her doors unlocked.
   a. naïve
   b. elevated
   c. boastful
   d. panoramic
   e. elated

127. Kinnel's re-election is being threatened by a growing _____ of disgruntled union members.
   a. rogue
   b. faction
   c. pariah
   d. guise
   e. anathema

128. The peasants passed their weary days in much _____ and little comfort.
  a. pertinence
  b. renown
  c. travail
  d. exile
  e. repose

129. Lyasia is a _____ of the clarinet; she has performed solos with many orchestras and bands around the world.
  a. neophyte
  b. novice
  c. virtuoso
  d. termagant
  e. plethora

130. The children knew that once their father made his decision, the new rule would be _____ because he would never change his mind.
  a. irrevocable
  b. articulate
  c. premeditated
  d. serried
  e. discourteous

131. The haunted house displayed _____ scenes in every room, causing squeamish visitors to scream.
  a. preparatory
  b. archaic
  c. macabre
  d. precocious
  e. impetuous

132. The concert audience was frustrated by the poor _____ of the sounds coming from the speakers.
  a. modulation
  b. recrimination
  c. terminus
  d. dissidence
  e. assertion

133. Please don't _____ me my success—I've worked hard to earn this promotion!
a. renege
b. begrudge
c. excise
d. staunch
e. vaunt

134. With an _____ blow of the whistle, the meddling parent interrupted the game to reiterate the rules of the tournament.
a. industrious
b. illustrious
c. eloquent
d. officious
e. enviable

135. The candidate's inappropriately sexist remark was met with a _____ of denunciations from the angry crowd.
a. bastion
b. fusillade
c. mélange
d. dichotomy
e. solecism

136. The _____ employee decided to complain publicly about the unacceptable working conditions.
a. discreet
b. prudent
c. precarious
d. malcontent
e. stupendous

137. The medicine man applied a sweet smelling _____ to the young brave's wounds.
a. triad
b. corrosive
c. parcel
d. unguent
e. pungent

138. The judge dismissed the extraneous evidence because it was not
_____ to the trial.
a. pertinent
b. pretentious
c. synonymous
d. abject
e. inalienable

139. The _____ nature of the song is supposed to be reminiscent of
shepherds calling to their flocks at night.
a. vocative
b. endemic
c. surreptitious
d. preternatural
e. inane

140. The _____ child caused great difficulties for her parents and
teachers because she refused to correct her bad behavior even in
the face of punishment.
a. adorable
b. sincere
c. incorrigible
d. lamentable
e. demure

141. The internist decided to treat the _____ with medication, but also
recommended rest and proper nutrition.
a. malady
b. nonentity
c. missive
d. repository
e. nonchalance

142. It was such a beautiful day that I decided to go for a _____ on my bike down to the local park.
  a. expedition
  b. jaunt
  c. pilgrimage
  d. repast
  e. intimation

143. The castaway's hut was _____ by the natives curious to see who the intruder was upon their island.
  a. beset
  b. surmised
  c. precluded
  d. garnered
  e. lauded

144. Sometimes my grandmother would _____ all different types of thread so she could include more colors in the clothes she sewed.
  a. daunt
  b. raddle
  c. scrabble
  d. thrush
  e. empower

145. The defense attorney's choice of words _____ that there were other possible versions of the crime, but the jury was unconvinced.
  a. pervaded
  b. insinuated
  c. discounted
  d. imposed
  e. ensconced

146. Ted's enthusiasm for becoming a professional drum player _____ when he realized he would have to practice several hours a day.
  a. waxed
  b. waned
  c. deranged
  d. flouted
  e. preempted

147. Some would say Muzak is a(n) _____ form of music, a kind of background noise designed to be heard but not listened to.
a. arable
b. degenerate
c. volatile
d. pivotal
e. exemplary

148. The teacher was dismissed for the _____ act of helping his students cheat on the exam.
a. steadfast
b. meritorious
c. unconscionable
d. pristine
e. fortuitous

149. The reformed criminal could not forget his guilty past; he was in a living state of _____.
a. perdition
b. tact
c. composure
d. principle
e. veracity

150. The _____ yoga instructor waited patiently for her students to find the proper pose, which she performed with ease.
a. unabashed
b. lissome
c. cosmopolitan
d. sneering
e. disparaging

Answers

126. **a.** *Naïve* (adj.) means lacking worldly experience; possessing a childlike innocence or simplicity.

127. **b.** A *faction* (n.) is a group or clique within a larger group, usually a minority, acting in unison in opposition to the larger group; internal dissension, conflict within an organization, nation, or other group.

128. **c.** *Travail* (n.) means hard or agonizing labor.

129. **c.** *Virtuoso* (n.) means a master in the technique of some particular fine art.

130. **a.** *Irrevocable* (adj.) means irreversible; not able to be revoked or recalled.

131. **c.** *Macabre* (adj.) means ghastly, horrible, or gruesome.

132. **a.** *Modulation* (n.) a regulation by or adjustment to a certain measure, such as in music or radio waves.

133. **b.** To *begrudge* (v.) means to envy the possession or enjoyment of; to give or allow with reluctance.

134. **d.** *Officious* (adj.) means marked by excessive eagerness in offering unwanted services or advice to others; unofficial.

135. **b.** A *fusillade* (n.) is a barrage; a rapid discharge of firearms, simultaneously or in rapid succession.

136. **d.** *Malcontent* (adj.) means dissatisfied, uneasy or discontent; a rebel.

137. **d.** An *unguent* (n.) is any soothing or healing ointment or lubricant for local application.

138. **a.** *Pertinent* (adj.) means applicable, related to the subject matter at hand.

139. **a.** *Vocative* (adj.) means pertaining to the act of calling.

140. **c.** *Incorrigible* (adj.) means bad to the point of being beyond correction; uncontrollable; impervious to change.

141. **a.** *Malady* (n.) is a disease or disorder.

142. **b.** A *jaunt* (n.) is usually a short journey taken for pleasure.

143. **a.** To *beset* (v.) means to surround on all sides; to annoy or harass persistently; to decorate with jewels.

144. **b.** To *raddle* (v.) means to twist together, to intertwine.

145. **b.** To *insinuate* (v.) is to hint or suggest; to intimate.

146. **b.** To *wane* (v.) means to diminish in intensity or size.

147. **b.** *Degenerate* (adj.) means having declined in quality or value, reduced from a former or original state, to degrade.

148. **c.** *Unconscionable* (adj.) means not restrained by conscience; unscrupulous.

149. **a.** *Perdition* (n.) the most modern use of the word means eternal damnation, or a hell.

150. **b.** *Lissome* (adj.) means lithe or lithesome, usually related to the body; moving or bending easily or limber.

Chapter 7

151. When we first meet Romeo, he is _____ over his unrequited love for Rosaline.
   a. brooding
   b. ogling
   c. meandering
   d. embellishing
   e. groveling

152. Because it had been worn and washed so often, Linus's favorite t-shirt was tattered and _____ with holes.
   a. salvaged
   b. circulated
   c. riddled
   d. emulated
   e. congregated

153. Henley's _____ remarks about my presentation did not bother me because I knew I'd done a good job.
  a. derogatory
  b. voracious
  c. tactile
  d. capricious
  e. amiable

154. Eels swim using a rapid _____ motion that propels them through the water.
  a. dissipating
  b. undulating
  c. eradicating
  d. objurgating
  e. irritating

155. Sick and tired of her boring job, Cecilia began to _____ what it would be like to quit.
  a. ponder
  b. disengage
  c. negate
  d. relinquish
  e. alleviate

156. The way my father likes to _____ with any salesperson to see if he can bargain for a lower price is embarrassing.
  a. striate
  b. variegate
  c. capitulate
  d. teem
  e. wrangle

157. The _____ construction crew built large new buildings all over the East Coast, wherever the demand for qualified workers took them.
  a. laconic
  b. irresolute
  c. itinerant
  d. parietal
  e. peremptory

158. The CEO's large expense accounts proved she was a _____ spender with the company's money.
a. injurious
b. ineffectual
c. liberal
d. malignant
e. insolvent

159. Daniela found the unchanging rhythm of the musical piece to be annoyingly _____.
a. recusant
b. monotonous
c. irreverent
d. coherent
e. redolent

160. The young, thin boy surprised his wrestling opponent with his _____ strength.
a. fraudulent
b. wiry
c. frolicsome
d. pretentious
e. endemic

161. The new actress's talents were severely _____ by the local critics; she went on to be a distinguished member of a well-respected acting company.
a. underrated
b. berated
c. placated
d. dissuaded
e. interred

162. To hide his insecurity, Barton often acted like a _____ so that he could make people laugh.
a. buffoon
b. martyr
c. neophyte
d. plebian
e. wraith

163. When Arnold's grandmother began to complain about the excruciating pain in her knees and legs, she was referred to an _____ specialist for a diagnosis.
a. optical
b. oral
c. archeological
d. osteopathic
e. psychological

164. Charlie's _____ behavior made it clear that he had been highly educated in matters of etiquette.
a. decorous
b. surreptitious
c. erratic
d. caustic
e. irksome

165. Staring at the _____ crystal blue water of the sea, Eileen thought she had never seen anything so beautiful.
a. flamboyant
b. appalling
c. devious
d. pristine
e. fiery

166. Wearing the designer's latest fashions, the _____ clothing model sashayed down the runway.
  a. jaunty
  b. tranquil
  c. fanatical
  d. recessive
  e. contemplative

167. Given his _____ nature, it was appropriate that he decided to be a trial lawyer after law school.
  a. lackluster
  b. engrossed
  c. penitent
  d. litigious
  e. obsolete

168. After her relationship ended, Patty, feeling _____, insisted on playing sad love songs repeatedly.
  a. infallible
  b. plausible
  c. formative
  d. mawkish
  e. persuasive

169. Sanji went abroad as a _____ young man; when he returned two years later, he seemed like an experienced man of the world.
  a. sardonic
  b. egalitarian
  c. reticent
  d. callow
  e. loquacious

170. Normally distinguished and reserved, Robert would act _____ when he joined his friends to cheer for their old high school team at annual the homecoming game.
a. indignant
b. oafish
c. poignant
d. reputable
e. obdurate

171. The protesters were concerned that the proposed legislation would have a(n) _____ effect on the state's nature preserves.
a. scintillating
b. deleterious
c. insipid
d. punctilious
e. parsimonious

172. Not swayed by his student's _____ flattery, the professor told him that his grade would not be changed.
a. forlorn
b. striated
c. undulating
d. unctuous
e. frowsy

173. Tonya found Isaac's public declarations of his love for her _____ and embarrassing.
a. necrotic
b. intriguing
c. witless
d. malodorous
e. pliant

174. The young kitten had a _____ look on its face when it noticed the menacing dog entering the yard.

    a. servile
    b. diligent
    c. scornful
    d. pavid
    e. optimistic

175. According to pirate lore, a terrible _____ would follow whoever opened the treasure chest.

    a. precursor
    b. precession
    c. rendition
    d. insurgence
    e. malediction

Answers

151. **a.** To *brood* (v.) is to be in deep thought, to think moodily or anxiously about something; to cover over, as with wings, in order to protect; to hang over, as of something threatening, dark, or menacing, to loom; to be silent or sullen, sulk; to sit on or hatch eggs.

152. **c.** To *riddle* (v.) means to pierce with many holes.

153. **a.** *Derogatory* (adj.) means tending to lessen in value, to detract or diminish; disparaging, belittling, injurious.

154. **b.** *Undulating* (adj.) means characterized by a wavelike motion.

155. **a.** To *ponder* (v.) is to weigh carefully in the mind.

156. **e.** To *wrangle* (v.) means to bicker, dispute, create a noisy argument.

157. **c.** *Itinerant* (adj.) means traveling from one place to another, usually on a planned course; working in one place for a short while before moving onto another place to work; wandering.

158. **c.** *Liberal* (adj.) means characterized by generosity or a willingness to give freely in large amounts; untraditional or broad-minded in beliefs.

159. **b.** *Monotonous* (adj.) means tediously lacking in variety; unvarying; repetitious.

160. **b.** *Wiry* (adj.) means thin, but tough and sinewy.

161. **a.** *Underrated* (adj.) means undervalued.

162. **a.** A *buffoon* (n.) is a ludicrous or bumbling person, a fool; someone given to clowning and amusing others through ridiculous behavior; a clown or jester.

163. **d.** *Osteopathic* (adj.) means a system of medicine pertaining to the bone and skeletal system.

164. **a.** *Decorous* (adj.) means characterized by good taste in manners and conduct, exhibiting propriety or decorum, proper.

165. **d.** *Pristine* (adj.) means pure, fresh and clean, as if new; original or primitive.

166. **a.** *Jaunty* (adj.) means sprightly in manner; stylish or smart in dress.

167. **d.** *Litigious* (adj.) means inclined to disagree or dispute, especially in lawsuits; argumentative.

168. **d.** *Mawkish* (adj.) means characterized by excessive sentimentality; overly emotional.

169. **d.** *Callow* (adj.) means lacking maturity or experience; immature, naïve.

170. **b.** *Oafish* (adj.) means acting stupid, goofy, or clumsy.

171. **b.** *Deleterious* (adj.) means having a harmful or adverse effect; destructive, hurtful, noxious.

172. **d.** *Unctuous* (adj.) means characterized by insincere earnestness; oily or fatty in appearance.

173. **c.** *Witless* (adj.) means foolish, indiscreet, or silly.

174. **d.** *Pavid* (adj.) means timid or fearful.

175. **e.** *Malediction* (n.) is a curse or a proclaiming of a curse against someone; an imprecation.

Chapter 8

176. A(n) _____ spirit only causes more stress and strife; it is better to forgive and forget.
   a. apathetic
   b. restorative
   c. flaccid
   d. vindictive
   e. fortuitous

177. When we were renovating the old house, we found a(n) _____ of $10 and $20 bills hidden inside the old laundry chute.
   a. odyssey
   b. matrix
   c. lament
   d. fodder
   e. cache

178. Even though the pilot promised it was safe, Neil was _____ to fly during a snowstorm.
a. habitual
b. overzealous
c. pavid
d. reluctant
e. salacious

179. Ron has few friends because he is _____ and cares only about himself.
a. mundane
b. intrepid
c. garrulous
d. voracious
e. egocentric

180. The workers attempted to _____ the supervisor's authority by negotiating terms with the clients themselves.
a. contradict
b. instigate
c. resonate
d. placate
e. undermine

181. The student failed his research paper because he chose to _____ material from a another author's work.
a. authorize
b. stimulate
c. overrule
d. plagiarize
e. meditate

182. The _____ old cowboy had a complexion that spoke of many years in the desert sun, rounding up wild horses.
a. secular
b. suave
c. turgid
d. wizened
e. truant

183. The swimmer's back injury _____ his prospects for a gold medal
at the world championship competition.
  a. compelled
  b. advanced
  c. jeopardized
  d. maintained
  e. expounded

184. As Ramiro strolled through his old neighborhood, he noticed
sounds and smells that were _____ of his childhood.
  a. belligerent
  b. malleable
  c. reminiscent
  d. recondite
  e. incessant

185. Lynette had to learn the _____ of the insurance profession before
she felt comfortable describing products to her clients.
  a. lexicon
  b. classicism
  c. juncture
  d. cessation
  e. asperity

186. Marta had to pay off her _____ to the credit card company before
she could get a mortgage.
  a. stipend
  b. liability
  c. remuneration
  d. concession
  e. consolidation

187. The local high school issued a _____ on field trips until the bus
was repaired; then traveling could begin again.
  a. indispensability
  b. divergence
  c. moratorium
  d. subjection
  e. compulsion

188. With Justine's _____ nature and passion for art, she would make an excellent tour guide for the museum.
a. volatile
b. congenial
c. servile
d. fledgling
e. trite

189. Patrice was a(n) _____ girl when she was teenager—long-limbed and constantly tripping over her own feet.
a. blithe
b. resolute
c. ungainly
d. preternatural
e. conducive

190. The employee's claim of being out with the flu did not seem very _____ because he returned from sick leave with a deep tan.
a. inattentive
b. inarticulate
c. tactful
d. plausible
e. vulnerable

191. The con man used his _____ to convince the elderly woman to sign over her life savings to him.
a. estuary
b. melee
c. flagrancy
d. malleability
e. wile

192. Mike proved to be _____ throw after throw, hitting the carnival dart game's bull's eye every time.
a. sedentary
b. temporal
c. mediocre
d. infallible
e. infeasible

193. Patrick, who was always joking, added _____ to the formal dinner, which his sedate employer did not appreciate.
   a. contemplation
   b. ordinance
   c. tutelage
   d. levity
   e. sincerity

194. Sunlight shining through a window was an obvious _____ in the nearly every one of the artist's works.
   a. disjunction
   b. hindrance
   c. repugnance
   d. motif
   e. variance

195. I like listening to Wesley go on about politics and social issues; his opinions are _____ with my own beliefs.
   a. latent
   b. explicit
   c. consonant
   d. ensconced
   e. rife

196. Most people will find the film silly and childish in its humor; the most _____ viewers will find it downright crass and offensive.
   a. servile
   b. petulant
   c. fastidious
   d. arcane
   e. boisterous

197. Even though he wanted to win the game, the coach felt that he would be _____ if he let the injured quarterback continue to play.
   a. contentious
   b. remiss
   c. erudite
   d. stringent
   e. reputable

198. The goal of any company is to have its product name become
_____—constantly at the forefront of the consumer's mind.
a. garrulous
b. unctuous
c. tremulous
d. ubiquitous
e. portentous

199. During the holiday season, the _____ theme is "Peace on Earth,
Goodwill Toward All."
a. mitigated
b. arrogant
c. controversial
d. prevalent
e. prestigious

200. Our cottage by the sea offers many days of relaxation with warm
sunshine and soothing _____.
a. zephyrs
b. dervishes
c. stanchions
d. ebbs
e. torques

Answers

176. **d.** *Vindictive* (adj.) means revengeful, hateful.

177. **e.** A *cache* (n.) is a hiding place for storing or concealing provisions or valuables; a secret store of valuables or money, a stash.

178. **d.** *Reluctant* (adj.) means unwilling to do what one is being called to do.

179. **e.** *Egocentric* (adj.) means caring only about or interested only in oneself or one's needs.

180. **e.** To *undermine* (v.) means to subvert in an underhanded way.

181. **d.** To *plagiarize* (v.) is to steal thoughts or words in literary composition.

182. **d.** *Wizened* (adj.) means withered or dry, especially with age.

183. **c.** *Jeopardize* (v.) means to put in jeopardy or at risk; a hazard or danger.

184. **c.** *Reminiscent* (adj.) means calling to mind or remembering.

185. **a.** *Lexicon* (n.) is the vocabulary used in a language, profession, class, or subject.

186. **b.** *Liability* (n.) is a debt or obligation; something for which one is liable.

187. **c.** *Moratorium* (n.) is a temporary suspension or postponement of a planned activity.

188. **b.** *Congenial* (adj.) means having a friendly or pleasant disposition, sociable; having similar tastes, habits, or temperament; suitable to one's needs or nature.

189. **c.** *Ungainly* (adj.) means clumsy or awkward.

190. **d.** *Plausible* (adj.) means apparently worthy of belief or praise.

191. **e.** *Wile* (n.) means an act or a means of cunning deception.

192. **d.** *Infallible* (adj.) means not fallible; completely trustworthy; certain.

193. **d.** *Levity* (n.) is an inappropriate lack of seriousness or lightness of manner; frivolity.

194. **d.** *Motif* (n.) is a recurrent theme or form in an artistic or literary work.

195. **c.** *Consonant* (adj.) means in agreement or accord, harmonious; having similar sounds.

196. **c.** *Fastidious* (adj.) means paying careful attention to detail, meticulous; difficult to please, exacting; extremely sensitive, squeamish, especially in regard to matters of cleanliness or propriety.

197. **b.** *Remiss* (adj.) means careless in performing duties.

198. **d.** *Ubiquitous* (adj.) means being present everywhere.

199. **d.** *Prevalent* (adj.) means widespread or widely accepted; predominant or extensive.

200. **a.** A *zephyr* is a soft, gentle breeze; a breeze that blows from the west.

Chapter 9

201. When Melinda arrived in the impoverished city, she was immediately _____ by bands of children begging for food.
  a. bedraggled
  b. accosted
  c. infiltrated
  d. rebuked
  e. exacerbated

202. According to the terms of the agreement, if Nicole defaulted on her loan, she would have to _____ her house and car, both which would become property of the bank.
  a. usurp
  b. evince
  c. debut
  d. forfeit
  e. stigmatize

203. Tony was tired of roommate's petty _____ about his personal life, so he moved out.
   a. appeasements
   b. quips
   c. quotas
   d. rallies
   e. iniquities

204. The food at the buffet table was a _____ array of delights that even the most disciplined dieter would find difficult to resist.
   a. tempestuous
   b. tantamount
   c. truculent
   d. temporal
   e. tantalizing

205. After fighting the five-alarm fire, the _____ firefighter could not relax enough to unwind and get some rest.
   a. amicable
   b. treacherous
   c. pliable
   d. durable
   e. overwrought

206. For years Henry bore the _____ of being the only man in five generations of his family not to make the varsity baseball team.
   a. stigma
   b. brunt
   c. treatise
   d. scintillation
   e. punctiliousness

207. Tabitha found an overpriced dining table at the antique shop and tried to _____ with the shopkeeper, but he refused to lower the price.
   a. haggle
   b. stipulate
   c. annunciate
   d. ruminate
   e. confer

208. The firefighter was _____ in the news for his heroic rescue of a child from a burning house.
   a. mandated
   b. inferred
   c. reconstituted
   d. augmented
   e. lauded

209. Although she was on a diet, Hannah intended to _____ in the feast of Thanksgiving.
   a. dilate
   b. enervate
   c. expunge
   d. nullify
   e. partake

210. The villagers locked their doors when they heard about the pirates who were _____ unprotected villages along the island's coastline.
   a. reforming
   b. marauding
   c. reclaiming
   d. conceding
   e. recapitulating

211. I could tell by Angelica's _____ tone that she was still very angry with me.
   a. ingratiating
   b. adjacent
   c. oblique
   d. acerbic
   e. eloquent

212. After years of living at a(n) _____ pace, Paola decided it was time to slow down and learn how to relax.
   a. frenetic
   b. pedestrian
   c. pretentious
   d. colloquial
   e. insipid

213. The hospital had an outbreak of chicken pox and was forced to _____ all patients and staff to prevent more infected victims.
   a. clandestine
   b. saturate
   c. germinate
   d. quarantine
   e. aggregate

214. Living on several acres of land dotted with oak and maple trees makes autumn leaf-raking a _____ task.
   a. fatuous
   b. toilsome
   c. tardy
   d. obsequious
   e. fawning

215. Acting in the high school play served to _____ Ander's appetite for professional acting.
   a. satiate
   b. whet
   c. purport
   d. incriminate
   e. corral

216. It would take many hours of cleaning and repairing for the young family to transform the _____ into a clean and comfortable little cottage.
   a. territory
   b. manor
   c. hovel
   d. demesne
   e. hacienda

217. Ms. Lu allowed her son a great deal of _____ in spending his birthday money, because she believed it should be his decision.
   a. injunction
   b. assimilation
   c. latitude
   d. declamation
   e. stimulus

218. It was once believed that alchemists could _____ common metals to gold.
   a. transmute
   b. commute
   c. execute
   d. repute
   e. denote

219. The close-up of the actor drinking the popular brand of cola in the movie was a _____ display of commercialism.
   a. dispassionate
   b. languid
   c. apathetic
   d. gratuitous
   e. unpunctual

220. Juneod was _____ after his alibi proved that he could not have committed the crime.
a. acquitted
b. protracted
c. derided
d. denounced
e. acquainted

221. This summer's movies are _____ for audiences of escape-the-heat mindless entertainment—not one film offers a substantive or even plausible plot.
a. privation
b. dulcet
c. jargon
d. fodder
e. germane

222. The dictator used propaganda and intimidation to _____ the revolution.
a. prelude
b. intimate
c. congregate
d. irradiate
e. quell

223. Standing on the _____, the preacher greeted the parishioners every Sunday morning.
a. steeple
b. pillar
c. parvis
d. manifestation
e. sensor

224. Simona's _____ with her money caught up with her when she
didn't have the resources to buy a badly needed new car.
a. miserliness
b. thriftiness
c. wantonness
d. intuition
e. predilection

225. The architect designed the ceiling using wood _____ that would
remain uncovered, creating a rustic ambience in the living room.
a. pediments
b. joists
c. mullions
d. banisters
e. abutments

Answers

201. **b.** To *accost* (v.) means to approach and speak to someone, usually in a bold and aggressive manner as with a demand.

202. **d.** To *forfeit* (v.) means to be deprived of or lose the right to by the act of a crime, offense, fault, breach, or error.

203. **b.** A *quip* (n.) is a sarcastic or cutting jest; a witty remark.

204. **e.** *Tantalizing* (adj.) means tempting, attractive, often via the senses.

205. **e.** *Overwrought* (adj.) means labored to excess; anxious, agitated.

206. **a.** *Stigma* means a mark of infamy or token of disgrace.

207. **a.** To *haggle* (v.) means to bargain, such as over a price, or dispute in a petty way; to wrangle.

208. **e.** To *laud* (v.) is to praise, honor, or glorify.

209. **e.** To *partake* (v.) is to have a share or take part.

210. **b.** To *maraud* (v.) is to rove and raid in quest of plunder.

211. **d.** *Acerbic* (adj.) means sour or bitter in taste; sharp or biting in tone, character, or expression.

212. **a.** *Frenetic* (adj.) means wildly excited or agitated, frenzied, frantic.

213. **d.** To *quarantine* (v.) means to restrict the entrance to and exit from any place under observation for infectious disease.

214. **b.** *Toilsome* (adj.) means laborious or hard work.

215. **b.** To *whet* (v.) means to make more keen or eager.

216. **c.** A *hovel* (n.) is a small crude house; a filthy or disorganized hut or shed.

217. **c.** *Latitude* (n.) is freedom from normal limitations or restraints in conduct; an angular distance from a plane of reference.

218. **a.** To *transmute* (v.) means to change in nature, substance, or form.

219. **d.** *Gratuitous* (adj.) means unjustified or unnecessary; of no cost.

220. **a.** To *acquit* (v.) means to free or clear from an accusation or charge; to release or discharge from a duty, obligation, or debt; to behave oneself in a certain manner.

221. **d.** *Fodder* (n.) is a consumable, often inferior resource or item, high in demand and usually abundant in supply.

222. **e.** To *quell* (v.) means to cease or suppress.

223. **c.** A *parvis* (n.) is the porch or area before a building (as a church).

224. **c.** *Wantonness* (n.) means recklessness; bawdy; merciless.

225. **b.** *Joist* (n.) is a small, horizontal beam that supports a ceiling or floor, usually made of wood, reinforced concrete, or steel.

Chapter 10

226. When the house on the corner burned down, the entire neighborhood _____ together to help to the victims re-establish their lives.
   a. rallied
   b. recited
   c. skulked
   d. disintegrated
   e. expedited

227. The massage therapist's _____ fingers quickly eased the tension in Blanche's back.
   a. deft
   b. furtive
   c. listless
   d. tentative
   e. blithe

228. Jade's parents were in _____ about the decision not to allow her to drive the family car to the prom; they both agreed that it would be unsafe.
   a. affluence
   b. redress
   c. refraction
   d. discord
   e. unison

229. As she walked through the halls of her old grade school, Madeline became _____, remembering her old friends and teachers.
   a. prolific
   b. nostalgic
   c. credulous
   d. precocious
   e. ambitious

230. After being cleared of all charges for slander, the attorney was able to go back to work and _____ his role as a prosecutor.
   a. inhibit
   b. reprimand
   c. remand
   d. resume
   e. dissipate

231. Ignacio's pain was so _____ that he called 911.
   a. remiss
   b. rapacious
   c. genteel
   d. resolute
   e. acute

232. The captain _____ the cargo to keep his ship afloat.
   a. rebuked
   b. listed
   c. disunited
   d. flanked
   e. jettisoned

233. The teacher tried to _____ her class of their dependence on the number lines pasted to the tops of their desks.
- **a.** wane
- **b.** wax
- **c.** whet
- **d.** wean
- **e.** wield

234. The young girl was so full of enthusiasm and _____ that she infected the room with energy.
- **a.** languidness
- **b.** apathy
- **c.** vivacity
- **d.** blandness
- **e.** tenacity

235. Ricky is a _____ of the local coffee shop; you can find him there just about every morning.
- **a.** diva
- **b.** relic
- **c.** denizen
- **d.** maverick
- **e.** pariah

236. The child danced with _____ joy at hearing the news that her father had arrived home from his lengthy business trip.
- **a.** staid
- **b.** unbridled
- **c.** stealthy
- **d.** beneficial
- **e.** restrained

237. Having never left the landlocked Midwest his entire life, Albert found that swimming in the ocean was quite a(n) _____.
- **a.** familiarity
- **b.** extrovert
- **c.** instinct
- **d.** novelty
- **e.** tabernacle

238. The rowdy crowd at the music concert _____ Herve, and he spilled his soda on his pants.
   a. jettisoned
   b. harrowed
   c. jostled
   d. lauded
   e. superceded

239. Known for his strong command of the courtroom, it was common knowledge that Judge Disantis considered outbursts from defendants to be _____.
   a. questionable
   b. objectionable
   c. antisocial
   d. pliable
   e. visionary

240. Blinded by _____, Nicholas accepted the job offer with the highest pay but the least possibility of making him happy.
   a. ennui
   b. heresy
   c. infamy
   d. avarice
   e. temperance

241. It was very unprofessional of you to _____ your assistant in front of everyone at the meeting; she deserves more respect, and any criticism of her performance should be done in private.
   a. placate
   b. augment
   c. usurp
   d. preclude
   e. deride

242. The log cabin had a(n) _____ feel, so it was often enjoyed by
   vacationers from the city throughout the year.
   a. abstract
   b. ersatz
   c. rustic
   d. raucous
   e. repellent

243. We knew Jana had _____ motives for running for class president:
   She wanted the nearby parking space that came with the office.
   a. anterior
   b. interior
   c. inferior
   d. posterior
   e. ulterior

244. The town board heard many outraged and _____ arguments from
   the citizens against the destruction of some wooded areas in order
   to build a new mall.
   a. tenuous
   b. vociferous
   c. vacuous
   d. satisfied
   e. egregious

245. The villainous gang's hideout was a den of _____ that no one
   would dare to enter.
   a. innocence
   b. habitants
   c. iniquity
   d. accolades
   e. innovation

246. Indigestion is a common _____ of participating in a hot-dog eating contest.
- **a.** euphemism
- **b.** penchant
- **c.** corollary
- **d.** juxtaposition
- **e.** itinerary

247. Although it was so ridiculous that no one believed it to be true, the reporter's _____ still cost the governor his re-election.
- **a.** hegemony
- **b.** sedition
- **c.** malaise
- **d.** compendium
- **e.** calumny

248. People on the street stopped to _____ over the artist's rendition of the Eiffel Tower, amazed by his ability to capture the detail.
- **a.** bedazzle
- **b.** innovate
- **c.** gratify
- **d.** counteract
- **e.** objectify

249. The veteran lieutenant was not happy with his _____ rank behind the two inexperienced men.
- **a.** tertiary
- **b.** silly
- **c.** unctuous
- **d.** superior
- **e.** fastened

250. The prime minister was admired by all, a(n) _____ even in an environment of corruption and disdain.
- **a.** admonishment
- **b.** alleviation
- **c.** nonpareil
- **d.** prototype
- **e.** profanation

Answers

226. a. To *rally* (v.) means to come together for a common purpose or as a means of support; to recover or rebound.

227. a. *Deft* (adj.) means quick and skillful in movement, adroit.

228. e. *Unison* (n.) means a condition of perfect agreement and accord.

229. b. *Nostalgic* (adj.) is sentimentally yearning for a point in the past.

230. d. To *resume* (v.) means to take up again after interruption.

231. e. *Acute* (adj.) means extremely sharp or intense; keenly perceptive or discerning; of great importance or consequence, crucial; also, having a sharp tip or point.

232. e. To *jettison* (v.) is to toss goods overboard to lighten the load of a ship or aircraft to improve stability; to toss off (a burden).

233. d. To *wean* (v.) means to detach someone from that to which he is accustomed or devoted.

234. c. *Vivacity* (n.) means liveliness, to be fill of life.

235. c. A *denizen* (n.) is one who frequents a particular place; one who lives in a particular place, an inhabitant.

236. b. *Unbridled* (adj.) means without restraint.

237. d. A *novelty* (n.) is a new or unusual thing or occurrence.

238. c. To *jostle* (v.) is to push or shove roughly against; to drive with pushing; to disturb or bump.

239. b. *Objectionable* (adj.) means unpleasant or offensive.

240. d. *Avarice* (n.) means an excessive or insatiable desire for material wealth; inordinate greed.

241. **e.** To *deride* (v.) is to speak of or treat with contempt; to ridicule scornfully.

242. **c.** *Rustic* (adj.) means rural; rough; made from rough limbs or trees.

243. **e.** *Ulterior* (adj.) means lying beyond or outside what is openly shown or said.

244. **b.** *Vociferous* (adj.) means making a loud outcry.

245. **c.** *Iniquity* (n.) is wickedness or overwhelming injustice.

246. **c.** *Corollary* (n.) means a natural consequence or result; a deduction or inference that follows from the proof of another proposition.

247. **e.** *Calumny* (n.) means a false statement or accusation uttered maliciously to harm another's reputation, slander.

248. **e.** To *objectify* (v.) means to stare at amorously.

249. **a.** *Tertiary* (adj.) ranking third in order of importance, position, or value.

250. **c.** A *nonpareil* (n.) is a person or thing of peerless excellence.

Chapter 11

251. The queen's _____ fell ill during his journey and was unable to negotiate on her behalf when he arrived at the economic summit.
a. penury
b. miscreant
c. emissary
d. denizen
e. zealot

252. Tai was _____ by a series of setbacks that nearly made him miss his deadline.
a. ensconced
b. relegated
c. beleaguered
d. solicited
e. winnowed

253. New York boasts many _____ restaurants—places that are elegant
and frequented by famous movie stars, political figures, and other
elite members of society.
a. pungent
b. posh
c. diminutive
d. mediocre
e. middling

254. Patsy was shocked to discover how much higher her IQ was than
the _____.
a. norm
b. stimulation
c. prudence
d. solitude
e. derivative

255. Although she appeared confident, once she began her speech, the
valedictorian's _____ voice indicated her nervousness.
a. supercilious
b. resonant
c. tenuous
d. placating
e. tremulous

256. Danielle cannot seem to find her niche in life; she has changed her
_____ at least three times in the past ten years.
a. automation
b. vocation
c. plethora
d. pliancy
e. combustion

257. The discovery of the new element was _____; the scientist was looking for something else.
a. insignificant
b. intrepid
c. eloquent
d. inadvertent
e. emollient

258. A charming painting of a pleasant _____ landscape hung above Vitaly's fireplace, in marked contrast to the noise and lights of the bustling city outside his window.
a. nascent
b. histrionic
c. bucolic
d. indigenous
e. ersatz

259. Aidan, who has always been painfully shy, was very _____ by the news that he would have to do a presentation in front of his classmates.
a. discomfited
b. circumvented
c. relegated
d. promulgated
e. castigated

260. Since his parents had little money, Peter was _____ to his uncle for paying for his college education.
a. alleged
b. provided
c. obliged
d. demented
e. fortified

261. With great _____, we stepped gingerly onto the planks of the dilapidated bridge that spanned a rocky stream twenty feet below.
a. trepidation
b. instigation
c. perdition
d. refraction
e. endowment

262. At the risk of sounding like an _____, the teacher assigned extra homework for the weekend.
a. oaf
b. ogre
c. impost
d. alcove
e. anathema

263. Felix felt that his mother's request to run her errands was a huge _____ since he would have rather watched a soccer match with his friends that afternoon.
a. justification
b. imposition
c. preponderance
d. deviation
e. recourse

264. The paper was _____ so that it could be easily removed from the bound notebook.
a. voracious
b. infectious
c. fickle
d. perforated
e. fluent

265. The mad scientist _____ the potion with acid, making it not only useless, but also dangerous.
a. corrugated
b. vitiated
c. implemented
d. instigated
e. titillated

266. Jayne's paintings were not minimalist, but they were _____, using only the most elemental and essential elements.
a. elliptical
b. truculent
c. pernicious
d. perfunctory
e. abstemious

267. Wendell's prolonged illness was the _____ that ignited his interest in science and led to his illustrious career in medical research.
a. hyperbole
b. catalyst
c. penchant
d. insolence
e. caveat

268. Stopping to admire the _____ in the front yard, the young woman continued on with her gardening duties.
a. paradigm
b. compost
c. clutter
d. oleander
e. patagium

269. The river, _____ with new-fallen rain, overflowed its banks and flooded the tiny village in a matter of hours.
a. placated
b. turgid
c. redundant
d. equivalent
e. quarantined

270. In a(n) _____ expression of pleasure, the infant clapped her hands and squealed with joy.

    a. overt
    b. obligatory
    c. illusive
    d. peremptory
    e. turbulent

271. Paula's _____ humor does not amuse many people; rather many find it offensive and hurtful.

    a. nebulous
    b. truncated
    c. stoic
    d. vitriolic
    e. flirtatious

272. The play's _____ debut was not a good sign for the struggling producer.

    a. unsubstantial
    b. inauspicious
    c. copious
    d. disembodied
    e. immaterial

273. At one time it was in _____ for women to wear gloves and hats whenever they were out in public.

    a. gore
    b. gauge
    c. vogue
    d. brawn
    e. vain

274. To ensure that Brenda wouldn't know where we were going for her birthday, I took the most _____ route I could think of.

    a. ardent
    b. craven
    c. enigmatic
    d. circuitous
    e. mercurial

275. The editorial was essentially a(n) _____ to the governor, praising her for her enactment of a series of environmental laws and for balancing the state budget for the first time in 20 years.

    a. juggernaut
    b. imprecation
    c. cabal
    d. oeuvre
    e. encomium

Answers

251. **c.** An *emissary* (n.) is an agent sent on a mission to represent the interests of someone else.

252. **c.** To *beleaguer* (v.) is to harass, beset, besiege.

253. **b.** *Posh* (adj.) means elegant and fashionable.

254. **a.** A *norm* (n.) is an average standard, pattern, or type.

255. **e.** *Tremulous* (adj.) means characterized by quivering or unsteadiness.

256. **b.** *Vocation* (n.) means a regular occupation or profession.

257. **d.** *Inadvertent* (adj.) means not attentive or heedless; acting carelessly; unintentional.

258. **c.** *Bucolic* (adj.) means of or characteristic of country life or people, rustic, especially in an idealized sense; of or characteristic of shepherds or herdsmen, pastoral.

259. **a.** To *discomfit* (v.) means to make uneasy, disconcert; to cause to lose one's composure; to break up or thwart the plans of, frustrate.

260. **c.** *Obliged* (v.) means to be indebted.

261. **a.** *Trepidation* (n.) means nervous uncertainty of feeling.

262. **b.** An *ogre* (n.) is, in popular usage, a cruel person, or a monster.

263. **b.** *Imposition* (n.) is the act of imposing something such as a burden or duty; an unfair demand.

264. **d.** *Perforated* (adj.) means with a line of holes to facilitate separation; pierced with a pointed instrument.

265. b. To *vitiate* (v.) means to spoil; to make faulty or impure; to corrupt morally.

266. a. *Elliptical* (adj.) means characterized by extreme economy of words or style; of, relating to, or having the shape of an ellipsis.

267. b. A *catalyst* (n.) is something that precipitates or causes a process or event; (in chemistry) a substance that initiates or accelerates a chemical reaction without itself being affected in the process.

268. d. An *oleander* (n.) is a beautiful but poisonous evergreen shrub.

269. b. *Turgid* (adj.) means swollen.

270. a. *Overt* (adj.) means apparent, obvious.

271. d. *Vitriolic* (adj.) means bitterly scathing; caustic.

272. b. *Inauspicious* (adj.) means not favorable or unfortunate; not promising success.

273. c. *Vogue* (n.) means the prevalent way or fashion.

274. d. *Circuitous* (adj.) means having or taking a roundabout, lengthy, or indirect course.

275. e. *Encomium* (n.) means a formal expression of praise, a glowing tribute.

Chapter 12

276. Claude felt particularly _____ as he carried the large satchel filled with cash through the dark streets to the bank.
   a. inclusive
   b. vulnerable
   c. reclusive
   d. unwieldy
   e. torrential

277. Niall's _____ attitude toward the boss is embarrassing; he does nearly everything for him except scratch his nose!
   a. subservient
   b. subversive
   c. subtle
   d. sundry
   e. surly

278. Although she was a successful professional, Debra's inability to accurately complete her taxes made her feel a bit _____.
a. endowed
b. rapturous
c. ravenous
d. obtuse
e. elated

279. Jeremy didn't want to appear _____, but his brothers simply could not convince him to change his mind.
a. pitiful
b. scrupulous
c. harmonious
d. obstinate
e. unabated

280. Buying homeowner's insurance is a wise decision because it provides _____ if your house should be damaged in a fire.
a. chastisement
b. indemnity
c. clarification
d. resolution
e. annulment

281. Although it was supposed to be written for the general public, the report was so _____ that only those with inside knowledge of government workings could understand it.
a. indigenous
b. ebullient
c. truculent
d. pugnacious
e. esoteric

282. Todd set up a rope to _____ the part of the exhibit that was off-limits.
   a. circumscribe
   b. laud
   c. efface
   d. undulate
   e. beguile

283. The loud clap of thunder caused the little dog to _____ all over.
   a. slather
   b. quake
   c. enunciate
   d. binge
   e. infuse

284. Francois fell into a groggy _____ after having suffered a high fever for several days.
   a. profundity
   b. sluggard
   c. verve
   d. stupor
   e. grovel

285. Blaine had a tendency to _____ certain details of his evenings out when he didn't want his parents to know where he had been.
   a. excel
   b. oscillate
   c. corroborate
   d. juxtapose
   e. omit

286. We took pity on the young _____ and brought him to a shelter where he could find food and warmth.
   a. waif
   b. perfidy
   c. ionic
   d. plaintiff
   e. troubadour

287. The fire caused _____ damage to the warehouse, which forced the owner to demolish the building.
a. sanctified
b. equitable
c. preliminary
d. irreparable
e. pretentious

288. When people are in love, they may find their beloved's _____— often annoying to or disparaged by others—to be charming and endearing.
a. foibles
b. mendacity
c. ennui
d. aplomb
e. penchants

289. Terreh was able to _____ the traffic jam by taking a series of one-way streets that led to the bridge.
a. staunch
b. diffuse
c. corroborate
d. circumvent
e. juxtapose

290. The risk of cheating on the test was not worth the possible _____ of failing the class.
a. specification
b. gratification
c. ramification
d. narcissism
e. renegade

291. We found that the gallons of water we had brought on our hike
were _____, and we had to carry the extra bottles home.
a. superannuated
b. extraordinary
c. derivative
d. superfluous
e. untenable

292. Moving all the heavy cinder blocks by hand from the driveway to
the backyard seemed like a(n) _____ task.
a. precipitous
b. poignant
c. onerous
d. salient
e. gallant

293. Claudia's _____ face gave no clue to her hard, cold heart.
a. winsome
b. gruesome
c. fatuous
d. ironic
e. flaccid

294. Keeping hot peppers in the olive oil _____ it with a spicy kick.
a. contemplates
b. stigmatizes
c. scrutinizes
d. infuses
e. defames

295. She realized mortgage rates had declined and decided it was
_____ to continue paying rent when she could now afford a
monthly payment for her own home.
a. referable
b. relative
c. subsequent
d. episodic
e. inexpedient

296. The deadline has been moved to this Friday, so we must _____ our efforts and complete the project earlier than we had planned.
a. wane
b. ruminate
c. burnish
d. pilfer
e. expedite

297. As the city grew and stretched its borders, it began to feel the _____ problems of urban sprawl and overpopulation.
a. improvident
b. mendacious
c. ersatz
d. concomitant
e. surreptitious

298. Terrance, a dentist, _____ to be with the media, so he could see the concert for free.
a. facilitated
b. conjugated
c. purported
d. tended
e. placated

299. _____ on a lounge chair by the pool was the very tan owner of the estate, relaxing in the midday sunshine.
a. Trident
b. Renegade
c. Fraught
d. Renowned
e. Supine

300. Observing his sister's _____ behavior of riding without a helmet, Jorge ran to get his mother.
a. contemptuous
b. contented
c. fictitious
d. parlous
e. pensive

Answers

276. **b.** *Vulnerable* (adj.) means assailable; capable of receiving injuries; open to attack.

277. **a.** *Subservient* (adj.) means following another's requests in a servantlike manner far below that which is called for.

278. **d.** *Obtuse* (adj.) means lacking quickness of perception or intellect.

279. **d.** *Obstinate* (adj.) means stubborn.

280. **b.** *Indemnity* (n.) is protection from loss or damage; immunity from punishment; compensation for loss or damage.

281. **e.** *Esoteric* (adj.) means designed for, confined to, or understandable only by a restricted number of people, an enlightened inner circle.

282. **a.** To *circumscribe* (v.) is to draw a line around, encircle; to restrict or confine; to determine the limits of, define.

283. **b.** To *quake* (v.) means to shiver or tremble, as from fear or cold; to shake or vibrate violently.

284. **d.** *Stupor* (n.) means profound lethargy, such as one might experience after being very ill.

285. **e.** To *omit* (v.) is to leave out; to neglect, disregard.

286. **a.** A *waif* (n.) is a stray; a homeless, neglected wanderer, especially a homeless child.

287. **d.** *Irreparable* (adj.) means not capable of being remedied or corrected; not reparable.

288. **a.** A *foible* (n.) is a minor weakness or character flaw; a distinctive behavior or attribute peculiar to an individual.

289. **d.** To *circumvent* (v.) is to go around, bypass; to get around or avoid through cleverness or artful maneuvering; to surround, enclose, entrap.

290. **c.** A *ramification* (n.) is a consequence for an action.

291. **d.** *Superfluous* (adj.) means extra; more than is needed, unnecessary.

292. **c.** *Onerous* (adj.) is burdensome or troublesome.

293. **a.** *Winsome* (adj.) means attractive.

294. **d.** To *infuse* (v.) is to instill or cause to penetrate; to inspire.

295. **e.** *Inexpedient* (adj.) means not expedient; not suitable or fit for the purpose; not tending to promote a proposed object.

296. **e.** To *expedite* (v.) means to speed up the progress of, accelerate; to process or execute quickly and efficiently.

297. **d.** *Concomitant* (adj.) means occurring or existing concurrently; accompanying, attendant.

298. **c.** To *purport* (v.) means to give false appearance of being.

299. **e.** *Supine* (adj.) means lying on the back.

300. **d.** *Parlous* (adj.) means dangerous, risky, or extreme.

Chapter 13

301. In an attempt to _____ the enemy, Braveheart rallied hundreds of fierce warriors.
   a. alienate
   b. scoff
   c. obliterate
   d. ostracize
   e. minimize

302. The film was completed on schedule despite the _____ circumstances regarding the location and extreme weather conditions.
   a. tenuous
   b. imperial
   c. cryptic
   d. contrived
   e. adverse

501 Sentence Completion Questions

303. The postcard advertised a free cruise to anyone who bought a magazine subscription, but after reading the fine print Sasha found the cruise was just a _____.
a. petition
b. gimmick
c. compromise
d. reference
e. motif

304. Many employers like to visit college campuses and _____ college seniors to work for their companies.
a. daunt
b. recruit
c. illuminate
d. dither
e. flout

305. I could tell by Konrad's _____ manner that he was really sorry for how he had treated Annette.
a. callous
b. erratic
c. zealous
d. nonchalant
e. contrite

306. The company officials felt the rising cost of health coverage was _____ enough to raise their employees' insurance premiums.
a. moratorium
b. justification
c. symbolism
d. disposition
e. habitude

307. The _____ of the sheriff's department ended at the county line.
a. prerequisite
b. emendation
c. alliteration
d. jurisdiction
e. respite

308. Ralph plays golf every chance he gets; even a weeklong golfing vacation could not _____ his appetite for the game.
   a. initiate
   b. satiate
   c. relinquish
   d. revive
   e. employ

309. We could not describe the scene before us; it was filled with such _____ beauty.
   a. inexorable
   b. unutterable
   c. uproarious
   d. mnemonic
   e. fretful

310. The subject matter was _____ because the mumbling professor spoke too quickly.
   a. obscure
   b. magnanimous
   c. treacherous
   d. vital
   e. maximized

311. Arnie becomes so _____ when he talks about painting that it is hard not to be infected by his enthusiasm.
   a. laconic
   b. circuitous
   c. impertinent
   d. ardent
   e. recalcitrant

312. The cruise ship's deliciously appetizing dinner buffets encouraged _____ among the vacationing passengers.
   a. gluttony
   b. squabbling
   c. equivocation
   d. restraint
   e. queries

313. As the pressures of her business became overwhelming, Charlotte chose to _____ her role as PTA president.
a. expedite
b. transgress
c. propagate
d. relinquish
e. retaliate

314. Don't let Julie's enthusiasm fool you; she's just a _____, not a professional dancer.
a. maverick
b. denizen
c. mercenary
d. maven
e. dilettante

315. Normally, Maya would not have made so many spelling mistakes in her essay; she is usually _____ about her spelling.
a. sumptuous
b. scurrilous
c. ridiculous
d. scrupulous
e. fatuous

316. It took four men two hours to move the _____ sofa up three flights of stairs into our apartment.
a. suave
b. garrulous
c. unwieldy
d. pivotal
e. quixotic

317. In the Roman myth, Artemis made a pilgrimage to the _____, hoping to learn the answer to her dilemma.
a. denouement
b. decorum
c. oracle
d. vizier
e. pillar

318. Orson was truly a(n) _____: towering over others at six feet nine inches, he was also one of the most influential and successful producers in the feature film industry.

   a. behemoth
   b. anathema
   c. demagogue
   d. viceroy
   e. charlatan

319. Brian was an _____ child, he was sent to the principal's office on numerous occasions for his rude classroom behavior.

   a. impeccable
   b. impertinent
   c. observant
   d. obscure
   e. adjuvant

320. The defendant waited anxiously for the jury to _____ the decision that would seal his fate.

   a. render
   b. deprecate
   c. rejuvenate
   d. disparage
   e. prohibit

321. We must _____ the information about the agenda changes immediately so that the conference attendees have time to adjust their schedules.

   a. burnish
   b. disseminate
   c. galvanize
   d. placate
   e. admonish

322. During the time of the plague in the little village, the forlorn
_____ of the church bells was an almost daily sound.
   a. prepossession
   b. premise
   c. delectation
   d. knell
   e. credence

323. If you can adhere to the _____ rules of a military society, the
Marines may be an excellent career choice.
   a. strident
   b. raucous
   c. stringent
   d. pedantic
   e. lurid

324. The natural _____ of the canyon cause it to be an everlasting
source of new adventures and beauty.
   a. blandishments
   b. vicissitudes
   c. mores
   d. platitudes
   e. nebulas

325. A life-long vegetarian, Xiomara _____ when she learned that the
sauce she'd just eaten was made with chicken broth.
   a. wavered
   b. blanched
   c. coalesced
   d. stagnated
   e. thwarted

Answers

301. **c.** To *obliterate* (v.) means to blot out or destroy.

302. **e.** *Adverse* (adj.) means acting against or contrary to; unfavorable; or opposed or opposing.

303. **b.** A *gimmick* (n.) is a tricky scheme or gadget.

304. **b.** To *recruit* (v.) means to seek to induct or enroll; to enlist.

305. **e.** *Contrite* (adj.) means feeling or expressing sorrow or regret for one's sins or offenses; penitent.

306. **b.** *Justification* (n.) is an explanation or reason that justifies or shows something to be necessary.

307. **d.** *Jurisdiction* (n.) is authority or power; sphere of power or authority.

308. **b.** To *satiate* (v.) means to satisfy fully the appetite or desire of.

309. **b.** *Unutterable* (adj.) means inexpressible.

310. **a.** *Obscure* (adj.) means not clearly expressed or easily understood; not easily seen or distinguished.

311. **d.** *Ardent* (adj.) means characterized by intense emotion or enthusiasm, passionate, fervent; glowing or burning like fire.

312. **a.** *Gluttony* (n.) is drinking or eating to excess; excessive indulgence.

313. **d.** To *relinquish* (v.) means to give up (something), renounce claim to.

314. **e.** A *dilettante* (n.) is an amateur, one who dabbles in an art or field of knowledge for amusement; a lover of fine arts, a connoisseur.

315. **d.** *Scrupulous* (adj.) means extremely careful, cautious in action for fear of doing wrong.

316. **c.** *Unwieldy* (adj.) means moved or managed with difficulty, as from great size or awkward shape.

317. **c.** An *oracle* (n.) is a person of great knowledge; the place where answers are given, as in a sanctuary.

318. **a.** A *behemoth* (n.) is a giant; something or someone who is enormous in size, power, or importance.

319. **b.** *Impertinent* (adj.) means improperly bold; rude; lacking good manners.

320. **a.** To *render* (v.) means to give in return in compliance with a duty; to make or depict.

321. **b.** To *disseminate* (v.) means to scatter widely, diffuse, spread abroad.

322. **d.** *Knell* (n.) is the sound of a bell ringing slowly for a funeral or death.

323. **c.** *Stringent* (adj.) means rigid, strict, or exacting.

324. **b.** *Vicissitudes* (n.) means a change, especially a complete change, of condition or circumstances.

325. **b.** To *blanch* (v.) means to turn pale, as if in fear; to take the color from, whiten.

Chapter 14

326. At the beginning of the ceremony, the high school band _____ the arrival of the graduates by playing the alma mater loudly and with enthusiasm.

    a. decried
    b. heralded
    c. permeated
    d. conjured
    e. thwarted

327. Although Sophie was afraid of heights, she seemed to have no _____ about driving over bridges.

    a. enormity
    b. qualms
    c. imminence
    d. resurrection
    e. severity

328. I will write a rough draft of the proposal, and then you can edit it for any _____ material so that it is as convincing and concise as possible.
    a. grandiose
    b. incontrovertible
    c. extraneous
    d. abysmal
    e. pensive

329. I had to call the repairman because the washing machine was off _____—it began making terrible sounds and failed to clean the clothes thoroughly.
    a. detriment
    b. preferment
    c. prevision
    d. kilter
    e. quandary

330. Minnie finally _____ to her sister's constant barrage of questions and revealed the identity of her new boyfriend.
    a. reiterated
    b. succumbed
    c. seceded
    d. reneged
    e. retaliated

331. The meeting is _____; everyone must attend.
    a. palatable
    b. compulsory
    c. reciprocal
    d. resilient
    e. ancillary

332. Through the _____ act of volunteering, it is possible to make a difference in the lives of the less fortunate.
  a. dilatory
  b. insurmountable
  c. diligent
  d. rapacious
  e. noble

333. The proposed design includes many _____ features that are not functional and can be eliminated to cut costs.
  a. jovial
  b. germane
  c. kinetic
  d. nonchalant
  e. extrinsic

334. Carly's _____ spending on shoes and clothing caused her parents a great deal of concern because she was no longer saving money for college.
  a. monotypic
  b. inconsistent
  c. perfunctory
  d. immoderate
  e. specious

335. The cop was in a _____: Should he chase the criminal or help the victim?
  a. quandary
  b. litany
  c. tatter
  d. discord
  e. plethora

336. The professor studied the _____ physics of ballet dancers and even published a study on the topic of dancers and movement.
a. creditable
b. kinetic
c. symbolic
d. prevalent
e. monotonous

337. Kyle was able to _____ the difficulties of an uncooperative staff, an impossible deadline, and a complicated project in order to present the report to the client.
a. surmount
b. dismount
c. retract
d. expel
e. intercede

338. Philbert's _____ manner fit in well with the atmosphere of the posh country club.
a. untoward
b. riotous
c. mundane
d. salacious
e. urbane

339. Elian tried his _____ on the wrong person, and it has finally landed him in jail.
a. clemency
b. jocularity
c. calamity
d. obsolescence
e. chicanery

340. There were several _____ buildings on the street, making it difficult for Margaret to determine which one was the dentist's office.
   a. nondescript
   b. transient
   c. impervious
   d. zealous
   e. impressionable

341. Inflated by his fans' _____, Evan lost sense of his small-town roots and began traveling with an entourage.
   a. inconstancy
   b. insolence
   c. haughtiness
   d. sufferance
   e. idolatry

342. To _____ a congressional bill, the president must use his official seal on all documents.
   a. nullify
   b. patronize
   c. victimize
   d. ratify
   e. mollify

343. The drama workshop's efforts _____ in the final production of a play written, directed, and acted by the students for the entire school.
   a. finalized
   b. languished
   c. teemed
   d. discerned
   e. culminated

344. There is no way around it: plagiarism is _____ to thievery.
   a. tantamount
   b. apathetic
   c. fatuous
   d. unscrupulous
   e. indecisive

345. For _____ deeds during her mission overseas, Tyesha was awarded the Congressional Medal of Honor.
   a. inept
   b. valorous
   c. erroneous
   d. malodorous
   e. benign

346. Adam read the employee manual so that he might _____ himself with his new responsibilities at the company.
   a. relinquish
   b. synthesize
   c. orient
   d. validate
   e. motivate

347. I am _____ of the problems that this solution will cause, but I still believe that this is the best possible solution.
   a. innocuous
   b. cognizant
   c. precipitous
   d. reminiscent
   e. belligerent

348. The spectacular presentation by a rainforest adventurer _____ Simon with the desire to travel to South America to see the jungles for himself.
   a. disheartened
   b. inhibited
   c. imbued
   d. reconstituted
   e. abhorred

349. When the senator's popularity suffered in the polls, he _____ his decision to raise taxes.
   a. recanted
   b. pulverized
   c. enveloped
   d. detracted
   e. extenuated

350. Because of the _____ of reliable information, Quentin's report was comprised mostly of speculation.
   a. dearth
   b. diatribe
   c. myriad
   d. juxtaposition
   e. tirade

Answers

326. **b.** To *herald* (v.) is to proclaim or announce; to foreshadow.

327. **b.** A *qualm* (n.) is a sudden or disturbing feeling.

328. **c.** *Extraneous* (adj.) means not vital or essential; not pertinent or relevant; coming from the outside or an outside source.

329. **d.** *Kilter* (n.) is order or good condition.

330. **b.** To *succumb* (v.) means to give in, cease to resist.

331. **b.** *Compulsory* (adj.) means obligatory, mandatory, required.

332. **e.** *Noble* (adj.) means having high, selfless moral standards; of excellent character.

333. **e.** *Extrinsic* (adj.) means not forming an essential part of a thing, extraneous; originating from the outside, external.

334. **d.** *Immoderate* (adj.) means excessive or extreme; exceeding reasonable limits.

335. **a.** A *quandary* (n.) is a difficult situation.

336. **b.** *Kinetic* (adj.) means pertaining to motion or caused by motion.

337. **a.** To *surmount* (v.) means to overcome by force of will.

338. **e.** *Urbane* (adj.) means characterized by refined manners; elegant or sophisticated.

339. **e.** *Chicanery* (n.) is trickery or sophistry used to deceive someone (especially to extract money).

340. **a.** *Nondescript* (adj.) means lacking any distinctive characteristics.

341. **e.** *Idolatry* (n.) is excessive reverence or adoration; the worship of idols.

342. **d.** To *ratify* (v.) means to make valid.

343. **e.** To *culminate* (v.) is to come to completion, end; to reach the highest point or degree, climax.

344. **a.** *Tantamount* (adj.) means equal to; having equal or equivalent value in terms of seriousness.

345. **b.** *Valorous* (adj.) means courageous, valiant.

346. **c.** To *orient* (v.) means to acquaint (oneself) with the existing situation or environment; determine one's position with reference to new ideas.

347. **b.** *Cognizant* (adj.) means fully knowledgeable or informed, conscious, aware.

348. **c.** To *imbue* (v.) is to inspire or pervade with ideas or feelings; to saturate with color; to permeate.

349. **a.** To *recant* (v.) means to renounce formally; to withdraw a former belief as erroneous.

350. **a.** *Dearth* (n.) means a severe shortage or scarce supply, especially of food; a lack of, insufficient quantity.

Chapter 15

351. Teachers should not only be knowledgeable but also _____;
students should feel comfortable approaching them with questions
or problems.
- **a.** wheedling
- **b.** patronizing
- **c.** laconic
- **d.** affable
- **e.** frugal

352. The pain medication Kristy received after surgery offered relief;
however, the overwhelming feeling of _____ was an unexpected
side effect, and she didn't like being groggy.
- **a.** extortion
- **b.** compellation
- **c.** acquisition
- **d.** affirmation
- **e.** lethargy

353. The ski lodge had a window that looked out upon a beautiful mountain _____.
   a. vista
   b. melee
   c. fray
   d. foray
   e. frieze

354. The palace's great hall was rich in history and splendor, the walls hung with _____ tapestries.
   a. mellifluous
   b. malleable
   c. prudent
   d. illusive
   e. ornate

355. After weeks of heavy rains, the earth gave way; mud and trees _____ down the mountain swallowing cars and houses in their path.
   a. ascended
   b. inculcated
   c. aspersed
   d. hurtled
   e. entreated

356. The _____ butter had been left in the refrigerator for years.
   a. complacent
   b. scandalous
   c. riveting
   d. dire
   e. rancid

357. Several weeks of extremely hot, dry weather _____ the land, so instead of rowing across a river, we walked across a cracked, parched riverbed.
   a. oscillated
   b. desiccated
   c. subverted
   d. coalesced
   e. thwarted

358. The pitcher's _____ workout regimen was the most grueling of all his teammates, and he never took a day off.
   a. Spartan
   b. spasmodic
   c. exclusive
   d. turgid
   e. truculent

359. Ethan's responses when he spoke on the telephone were _____ and he nearly always made his customers think he was rude.
   a. receptive
   b. laconic
   c. uncanny
   d. suave
   e. ponderous

360. I was bored with the _____ conversation of my roommates and longed for some intellectual stimulation.
   a. egregious
   b. pronounced
   c. vapid
   d. intriguing
   e. exonerating

361. Ned's fear was _____ as he watched the 60-foot waves approach his little boat.
   a. futile
   b. genteel
   c. innovative
   d. palpable
   e. detrimental

362. Moving swiftly and gracefully through the backyard, the cat suddenly _____ when she hit the thorny bush.
   a. recoiled
   b. recuperated
   c. invigorated
   d. fabricated
   e. throttled

363. Although others were fooled by "Doctor" Winston's speech, Lily knew him for what he was: a(n) _____.

    a. panacea

    b. charlatan

    c. prevarication

    d. accolade

    e. primadonna

364. The task of building the cabin was a _____ one, but Rob was up to the challenge.

    a. laborious

    b. venerable

    c. archaic

    d. cynical

    e. unbiased

365. After the neighbor's stereo woke her up for the fifth night in a row, Brenda felt _____ to complain.

    a. impelled

    b. rebuked

    c. augmented

    d. implicated

    e. destined

366. Carter is writing a letter of recommendation that I can include in my _____ for prospective employers.

    a. denunciation

    b. panacea

    c. dossier

    d. incantation

    e. restitution

367. _____ laughter came from the upstairs apartment where Trang was having a graduation party.

    a. Scurrilous

    b. Deleterious

    c. Fatuous

    d. Uproarious

    e. Malicious

368. In the middle of his eloquent _____, the audience suddenly broke into applause.
a. ovation
b. oration
c. inclination
d. provocation
e. illusion

369. I like the _____ style of these essays; they make complex issues accessible by presenting them in everyday language.
a. colloquial
b. obsolete
c. pristine
d. exacting
e. furtive

370. A diamond ring is the _____ symbol of love and affection.
a. precocious
b. fugacious
c. supplemental
d. quintessential
e. barbarous

371. Allen's _____ distanced him from his family, but he was still unwilling to apologize.
a. regeneration
b. contingency
c. equivalence
d. impenitence
e. innovation

372. Nothing will _____ my memory of the night we first met; the images are forever burned in my mind.
a. appease
b. undulate
c. inculcate
d. efface
e. truncate

373. With the curtains drawn back, the room was _____ with warm sunlight.
a. recessed
b. intruded
c. suffused
d. belied
e. taut

374. The devastating drought forced the _____ tribes of the rainforest to leave their homes and venture into the modern world.
a. indigenous
b. puritanical
c. indigent
d. imminent
e. munificent

375. Jason's _____ approach to management included narrowing the salary gap between the CEOs and office workers.
a. stoic
b. apathetic
c. utilitarian
d. endemic
e. proactive

Answers

351. **d.** *Affable* (adj.) means easy and pleasant to speak to, approachable; friendly, warm, gracious.

352. **e.** *Lethargy* (n.) is the state of drowsiness or sluggish inactivity.

353. **a.** *Vista* (n.) means a view or prospect.

354. **e.** *Ornate* (adj.) means richly and artistically finished or stylized.

355. **d.** To *hurtle* (v.) is to rush with great speed; to move violently with great noise; to fling forcefully.

356. **e.** *Rancid* (adj.) means rotten or putrid.

357. **b.** To *desiccate* (v.) means to dry out thoroughly, become dry; to make dry, dull, or lifeless.

358. **a.** *Spartan* (adj.) means rigorously severe (from the Greek city-state Sparta known for its austere and rigid lifestyle); marked by strict self-discipline; characteristically simple or frugal.

359. **b.** *Laconic* (adj.) means curt, concise, but expressing much in a few words; brief and to the point.

360. **c.** *Vapid* (adj.) means dull, lacking life, sprit or substance; tedious.

361. **d.** *Palpable* (adj.) means tangible, noticeable; easily perceived and detected.

362. **a.** To *recoil* (v.) means to jump back suddenly.

363. **b.** A *charlatan* (n.) is someone who makes elaborate, fraudulent claims to having certain skills or knowledge; a quack, imposter, fraud.

364. **a.** *Laborious* (adj.) means characterized by hard work, exertion, or perseverance.

365. **a.** To *impel* (v.) is to motivate; push or drive forward; propel.

366. **c.** A *dossier* (n.) is a collection of papers giving detailed information about a particular person or subject.

367. **d.** *Uproarious* (adj.) means noisy.

368. **b.** An *oration* (n.) is a formal speech for a special occasion.

369. **a.** *Colloquial* (adj.) means characteristic of informal spoken language or conversation; conversational.

370. **d.** *Quintessential* (adj.) is the best and purest part of a thing; the most typical example of a thing.

371. **d.** *Impenitence* (n.) is the trait of refusing to repent; unwilling to show regret for wrongdoing.

372. **d.** To *efface* (v.) means to rub out, erase; to cause to dim or make indistinct; to make or conduct oneself inconspicuously.

373. **c.** To *suffuse* (v.) means to cover or fill the surface of, as in to fill with light.

374. **a.** *Indigenous* (adj.) means originating or being native to a specific region or country; also inherent or natural.

375. **c.** *Utilitarian* (adj.) means related to the ethical doctrine that actions are right because they are useful or beneficial to the greatest number of people.

Chapter 16

376. If people continue to _____ the rainforests, soon they will disappear from the earth.

    a. dominate

    b. frolic

    c. laminate

    d. neglect

    e. provoke

377. My parents always seem to worry and _____ more about money when tax season is approaching.

    a. proximate

    b. quibble

    c. supplicate

    d. dabble

    e. alienate

378. While the king and the members of his court lived in the most opulent luxury, the peasants in his kingdom lived in the most _____ poverty.
   a. abject
   b. incessant
   c. relinquished
   d. erratic
   e. lugubrious

379. Samantha had an _____ trust in her grandfather, who was an honorable man and kind to everyone he met.
   a. implicit
   b. insecure
   c. irreverent
   d. irresolute
   e. astringent

380. Antonello searched the forest around his campsite for small branches to _____ the fire, so he could eventually cook his dinner.
   a. stifle
   b. kindle
   c. suppress
   d. dissipate
   e. prohibit

381. Although I meant it as a compliment, Zander _____ my remark as an insult.
   a. construed
   b. eradicated
   c. truncated
   d. permeated
   e. redacted

382. The sailor's _____ complexion bespoke his many sunny days at the lookout post.
a. swarthy
b. syncopated
c. pallid
d. wan
e. pasty

383. Tanya is a _____ person, trusted by all who know her.
a. porous
b. voracious
c. spurious
d. specious
e. veracious

384. After the third relative was hired to an upper-level position, several people quit the company, claiming that _____ caused a decline in employee morale.
a. carrion
b. explicitness
c. skepticism
d. devotion
e. nepotism

385. Genevieve's stunning debut performance at the city opera has earned her _____ from some of the city's toughest critics.
a. antipathy
b. insinuations
c. destitution
d. lamentations
e. accolades

386. The shaggy neon couch was a(n) _____ in the conservative room decorated with earth tones.
a. incongruity
b. insinuation
c. temerity
d. reiteration
e. intonation

387. Harris tried to _____ his fear of flying when he boarded the plane, but he could not curb his anxiety.
a. accelerate
b. expound
c. maximize
d. employ
e. repress

388. Gabi found that whenever she was confused about an idea or issue, writing about it would help _____ her true feelings.
a. vacillate
b. elucidate
c. wheedle
d. deprecate
e. indoctrinate

389. After the powerful windstorm, Marie discovered a splintered and fallen tree limb had _____ the vinyl lining of her swimming pool.
a. extenuated
b. calculated
c. retaliated
d. lacerated
e. curtailed

390. Johnny's good behavior in class yesterday was _____ by his disruptive outbursts in Math this morning.
a. abated
b. negated
c. reiterated
d. mandated
e. nominated

391. Jason and Joshua made _____ plans to meet in the cafeteria to study for the test, provided Jason's class ended on time.
a. beguiling
b. tenuous
c. assured
d. tentative
e. promotional

392. The professor's lectures were filled with excessive _____, lasting much longer than was necessary to convey his ideas.
   a. verbiage
   b. herbage
   c. maliciousness
   d. portent
   e. intrigue

393. Ming's blatant lie revealed that he suffered no _____ about being dishonest to his parents.
   a. compunction
   b. repudiation
   c. vindication
   d. evanescence
   e. veracity

394. Diane, always teasing, was known for her _____ , but as a result, nobody knew when to take her seriously.
   a. jocularity
   b. servitude
   c. logic
   d. austerity
   e. inclemency

395. "Absolute power corrupts absolutely," said Haines. "There is no such thing as a(n) _____ who is not a corrupt and cruel ruler."
   a. imbroglio
   b. pedant
   c. despot
   d. agnostic
   e. archetype

396. During his _____ in office the mayor made several controversial decisions about city planning.
   a. treatise
   b. integration
   c. teem
   d. flout
   e. tenure

397. Recovering from the tragedy, Helena found the _____ sunrise
reassuring, as it gave her something to rely on each and every
morning.
a. hidden
b. clairvoyant
c. cognizant
d. deft
e. quotidian

398. Flaws in Claire's opponent's chess game showed him to be _____,
and Claire knew her victory was assured.
a. predatory
b. indistinguishable
c. ornery
d. vincible
e. resolute

399. The ad didn't mention a specific salary; it just said "compensation
_____ with experience."
a. compulsory
b. manifest
c. prolific
d. commensurate
e. precluded

400. The _____ she felt for shopping made it impossible for her to
walk by a sale window without stopping.
a. providence
b. blunder
c. omission
d. repulsion
e. estrus

Answers

376. **d.** To *neglect* (v.) means to be careless about; to fail to care for or to do; to be remiss about.

377. **b.** To *quibble* (v.) means to find fault or criticize for petty reasons.

378. **a.** *Abject* (adj.) means wretched, degraded, debased; of the most contemptible or miserable kind; showing utter resignation or humiliation, groveling, servile.

379. **a.** *Implicit* (adj.) means unquestioning or trusting without doubt; understood rather than directly stated; implied.

380. **b.** *Kindle* (v.) means to cause to burn with flames; to ignite; to set on fire.

381. **a.** To *construe* (v.) is to interpret or understand; to make sense of, explain the meaning of.

382. **a.** *Swarthy* (adj.) means having a dark hue, especially a dark or sunburned complexion.

383. **e.** *Veracious* (adj.) means truthful, honest; habitually disposed to speak the truth.

384. **e.** *Nepotism* (n.) is favoritism for kin when conferring jobs, offices, or privileges.

385. **e.** An *accolade* (n.) is an award or special acknowledgement signifying approval or distinction.

386. **a.** *Incongruity* (n.) is the quality of being inappropriate or unbecoming; not consistent in character.

387. **e.** To *repress* (v.) means to keep under or restrain; to curb or subdue.

388. **b.** To *elucidate* (v.) means to make clear or manifest; to free from confusion or ambiguity.

389. **d.** To *lacerate* (v.) is to rip, tear, or mangle.

390. **b.** To *negate* (v.) means to nullify, invalidate, or deny.

391. **d.** *Tentative* (adj.) means provisional or uncertain; not fixed or set.

392. **a.** *Verbiage* (n.) means the use of many words without necessity.

393. **a.** *Compunction* (n.) means a feeling of uneasiness or regret caused by a sense of guilt, remorse; a pang of conscience at the thought or act of committing a misdeed.

394. **a.** *Jocularity* (n.) is the state of being jocular, which is characterized by joking or jesting.

395. **c.** A *despot* (n.) is someone who rules with absolute power; a dictator or tyrant.

396. **e.** *Tenure* (n.) means the term during which a thing is held; often used in connection with career positions.

397. **e.** *Quotidian* (adj.) means occurring or returning daily.

398. **d.** *Vincible* (adj.) means conquerable, capable of being defeated or subdued.

399. **d.** *Commensurate* (adj.) means corresponding in size, degree, or extent; proportionate.

400. **e.** An *estrus* (n.) is an irresistible impulse or passion.

Chapter 17

401. The owners of the bed-and-breakfast were extremely _____ to their guests, who enjoyed elegant meals, prompt service, and beautifully decorated rooms.
   a. hospitable
   b. hostile
   c. remiss
   d. gallant
   e. indomitable

402. Homeless people often lead a(n) _____ lifestyle because they repeatedly get uprooted from the streets and alleys where they live.
   a. aristocratic
   b. platonic
   c. analytic
   d. nomadic
   e. ballistic

403. Linda's _____ for picking the right stocks made her a very
wealthy woman.
   a. knack
   b. reception
   c. rendition
   d. impropriety
   e. concourse

404. Computers and word processing software have made the art of
hand-writing letters virtually _____.
   a. barren
   b. boisterous
   c. obsolete
   d. dignified
   e. relevant

405. Marco has an irresistibly _____ manner that many young women
find charming and attractive.
   a. obstinate
   b. staid
   c. bland
   d. supple
   e. suave

406. Chantel kept the _____ of her beloved foremost in her mind as
she traveled to countries far and wide in her quest to find him.
   a. prelude
   b. armistice
   c. hirsute
   d. presage
   e. visage

407. The cozy beach cottage was only _____ for summer tenants
because it lacked the insulation to make a winter stay comfortable.
   a. stagnant
   b. erroneous
   c. resilient
   d. habitable
   e. ineffective

408. The settlers decided to build their town at the _____ of two
rivers; that settlement became the city of Pittsburgh.
a. veneer
b. lexicon
c. hiatus
d. tirade
e. confluence

409. Furious that Lou had lied about his references, Noi _____ her
decision to promote him to assistant manager.
a. elevated
b. incriminated
c. complied
d. rescinded
e. fortified

410. To prove your theory, you need to design an experiment that will
provide _____ evidence.
a. perfunctory
b. elusive
c. noxious
d. empirical
e. lamentable

411. Rachel's mother was appalled by the amount of _____ humor on
television during hours when young children were still awake.
a. fraudulent
b. senile
c. proportional
d. lascivious
e. laborious

412. The scared boy on the roller coaster made sure his seatbelt was
_____ across his body.
a. slack
b. taut
c. trite
d. striated
e. curt

413. The female fox's _____ over her burrow indicates that she has just birthed her young.
   a. vendetta
   b. preening
   c. vigilance
   d. sepulcher
   e. rendezvous

414. After Ginger banged her head, she noticed that a large lump began to _____ from her forehead.
   a. invade
   b. provoke
   c. sustain
   d. obtrude
   e. elevate

415. The devoted fans paid _____ to the late singer by placing flowers on his memorial and by holding burning votive candles.
   a. tariffs
   b. accouterment
   c. retrospection
   d. appraisement
   e. homage

416. Losing his entire business to the flood, Bill's only _____ was to file bankruptcy.
   a. dross
   b. enigma
   c. fervor
   d. imprecation
   e. recourse

417. The new evidence convinced the District Attorney to overturn Martin's conviction and _____ him.
   a. appropriate
   b. truncate
   c. elucidate
   d. exonerate
   e. protract

418. Christopher hired a tree-trimming crew to cut the _____ branches of the pine tree that were scraping the side of his house.
a. fastidious
b. lateral
c. nebulous
d. abject
e. recessive

419. We both knew our summer romance was _____ , and we would just be memories in each other's minds by the winter.
a. restorative
b. tempting
c. temporal
d. understated
e. indecisive

420. The dissatisfied workers spread their _____ attitudes among themselves until there was a danger of a full-scale rebellion against the owners of the factory.
a. paradoxical
b. monochromatic
c. benign
d. virulent
e. portentous

421. The junkyard was littered with _____ objects, making it unsightly to the neighborhood behind it.
a. otiose
b. obtuse
c. jovial
d. decorative
e. buoyant

422. Although Maya's _____ sensibilities are quite different from mine, I think she is a remarkable interior decorator and I recommend her highly.
a. aesthetic
b. dialectical
c. reclusive
d. synthetic
e. mercurial

423. The meticulous art student arranged her paint colors by a darkening _____ on her palette.
a. limitation
b. gradation
c. moratorium
d. juncture
e. tincture

424. J.P. recalled running through the _____ of tall rows of corn stalks that dominated his grandfather's summer garden.
a. terminals
b. temperament
c. labyrinth
d. basin
e. deference

425. Peter displayed an air of _____ when the officer asked him if he knew the speed limit.
a. omniscience
b. obstinacy
c. nescience
d. obstetrics
e. platitude

Answers

401. **a.** *Hospitable* (adj.) means treating guests kindly and generously; being agreeable, receptive or of an open mind.

402. **d.** *Nomadic* (adj.) means roaming from place to place or wandering.

403. **a.** *Knack* (n.) is a natural talent; a clever way of doing something.

404. **c.** *Obsolete* (adj.) means antiquated, disused; discarded.

405. **e.** *Suave* (adj.) means having a smooth and pleasant manner.

406. **e.** *Visage* (n.) means the face, countenance, or look of a person.

407. **d.** *Habitable* (adj.) means acceptable for inhabiting.

408. **e.** *Confluence* (n.) means a flowing or coming together; a gathering or meeting together at a point or juncture; a place where two things come together, the point of juncture.

409. **d.** *Rescinded* (v.) means revoked.

410. **d.** *Empirical* (adj.) means relying on, derived from, or verifiable by; experimental or observational rather than theory.

411. **d.** *Lascivious* (adj.) means lewd, lustful, or wanton.

412. **b.** *Taut* (adj.) means stretched tight.

413. **c.** *Vigilance* (n.) means alert and intent mental watchfulness in guarding against danger.

414. **d.** To *obtrude* (v.) means to stick out, push forward.

415. **e.** *Homage* (n.) is respect paid publicly; reverence rendered; deference.

416. **e.** *Recourse* (n.) means a last option or way out.

417. **d.** To *exonerate* (v.) means to free from blame or guilt, absolve; to release from a responsibility or obligation, discharge.

418. **b.** *Lateral* (adj.) means pertaining to or extending from the side.

419. **c.** *Temporal* (adj.) means enduring for a short time; transitory.

420. **d.** *Virulent* (adj.) means exceedingly noxious, deleterious, or hateful.

421. **a.** *Otiose* (adj.) means needless, functionless; unemployed or useless.

422. **a.** *Aesthetic* (adj.) means concerning or characterized by an appreciation of beauty or good taste; characterized by a heightened sensitivity to beauty, artistic.

423. **b.** *Gradation* (n.) is the changing of a color, shade, or tint to another by gradual degrees; the process of bringing to another grade in a series; a stage or degree in such a series.

424. **c.** *Labyrinth* (n.) is a maze of paths or a complicated system of pathways in which it is challenging to find the exit; something extremely complex in structure or character.

425. **c.** *Nescience* (n.) is ignorance, or the absence of knowledge.

Chapter 18

426. I have tried for years to get close to my brother Rae, but he has always remained _____.
   a. cognizant
   b. assiduous
   c. vociferous
   d. aloof
   e. accommodating

427. In his later years, the once wildly successful gambler lost his fortune, and became a homeless _____ on the streets of Las Vegas.
   a. granger
   b. miser
   c. strategist
   d. vagabond
   e. speculator

428. _____ animals are able to survive easily in the wilderness because, for example, they can live on berries or insects.
a. Omnipotent
b. Omnivorous
c. Luminous
d. Lavish
e. Precarious

429. Sally had planted the seeds in the greenhouse three weeks ago; they would begin to _____ any day now.
a. germinate
b. revolve
c. tint
d. ratify
e. modulate

430. Julia's parents gave her one _____ regarding her new job: It could not interfere with her schoolwork.
a. procession
b. consensus
c. manifestation
d. provision
e. reprieve

431. Despite enthusiastic efforts from the supporting cast, the critics agreed the star of the play gave a _____ performance, ruining the chance of lucrative box office sales.
a. infallible
b. vigorous
c. victorious
d. felicitous
e. lackluster

432. The tenor's _____ voice filled the concert hall.
a. sinuous
b. timid
c. tenuous
d. sonorous
e. striated

501 Sentence Completion Questions

433. After the fire, there were ashes in every _____ of the old farmhouse.
a. belfry
b. reprieve
c. tangent
d. orifice
e. tribunal

434. Luanne experiences serious _____ whenever she climbs several flights of steep stairs.
a. vertigo
b. inebriation
c. exoneration
d. fallacy
e. plethora

435. The _____ of the successful product idea was attributed to the extraordinarily creative company president.
a. demise
b. genesis
c. symmetry
d. repletion
e. dominion

436. When the company reached it's _____ of hiring one hundred college graduates, they proceeded to recruit older, more experienced candidates.
a. quota
b. hybrid
c. detriment
d. fiasco
e. malady

437. After her extended illness, Delia experienced a long period of
_____ when she did not want to work, exercise, or clean.
a. languor
b. arrogance
c. insolence
d. forethought
e. recompense

438. Floyd has a distinctive _____ to his voice—easily recognizable
over the phone.
a. viscosity
b. brawn
c. timbre
d. diadem
e. ingenuity

439. The house was consumed in flames and not a _____ of it
remained after the fire.
a. vestige
b. visage
c. vestibule
d. vicissitude
e. viceroy

440. David felt as if the family picnic would be a(n) _____ time to talk
with his grandmother about her plans for the holidays.
a. opportune
b. disastrous
c. unctuous
d. trite
e. surly

441. The children were _____ for eating the whole batch of cookies
before dinner.
a. indignant
b. belittled
c. chagrined
d. eluded
e. admonished

442. During his routine, the stand-up comic refused to be shaken by the heckler who _____ him every few minutes.
a. ignored
b. abetted
c. enforced
d. gibed
e. cited

443. Going away for spring break was not in the _____ of possibility, since neither Helga nor Olga had any money.
a. fascism
b. fulcrum
c. introversion
d. realm
e. nadir

444. Oscar _____ his sister not to tell their mother what he had done, for he knew his punishment would be severe.
a. beguiled
b. vied
c. exhorted
d. maligned
e. corroborated

445. _____ were in order as James performed brilliantly on stage in his first role as an understudy.
a. Pathos
b. Ignominies
c. Kudos
d. Subsidies
e. Statutes

446. The Boston Tea Party happened because the Americans believed the British tea taxes were _____ the rights of the colonists.
a. trespassing
b. reviling
c. sublimating
d. transgressing
e. entreating

447. The old bridge's steel _____ were rusty and in need of repair.
   a. piers
   b. campaniles
   c. manacles
   d. girders
   e. spindles

448. The budding flowers, warm breezes, and birth of young animals
   suggest the much-welcomed _____ atmosphere in the country
   after a long, hard winter.
   a. venial
   b. menial
   c. venal
   d. vernal
   e. verbal

449. Since she had not exercised in five years, Margarita attempt to jog
   five miles on her first day of cardio-training was a little _____.
   a. pessimistic
   b. irrelevant
   c. trivial
   d. quixotic
   e. relieved

450. The legal internship program was developed under the _____ of
   the district attorney's office.
   a. bastion
   b. propensity
   c. aegis
   d. faction
   e. cacophony

Answers

426. **d.** *Aloof* (adj.) means physically or emotionally distant; reserved, remote.

427. **d.** A *vagabond* (n.) is a wanderer; a person who does not have a permanent home.

428. **b.** *Omnivorous* (adj.) means feeding on both animal and vegetable substances; having an insatiable appetite for anything.

429. **a.** To *germinate* (v.) means to begin to grow or sprout; to cause to come into existence or develop.

430. **d.** A *provision* (n.) is a stipulation or qualification; a stock of supplies.

431. **e.** *Lackluster* (adj.) means lacking liveliness or brightness; dull.

432. **d.** *Sonorous* (adj.) means producing sound; impressive or grand in effect.

433. **d.** An *orifice* (n.) is an opening, a hole; a perforation; a mouth or hole through which something may pass.

434. **a.** *Vertigo* (n.) is dizziness often caused by experiencing heights.

435. **b.** *Genesis* (n.) is the origin, beginning, or foundation; the act of forming something new; the first event in a series of events.

436. **a.** A *quota* (n.) is a proportional share.

437. **a.** *Languor* (n.) is a lack of energy or interest; a feeling of being without spirit; sluggishness.

438. **c.** *Timbre* (n.) is the quality of a tone, as distinguished from intensity and pitch.

439. **a.** *Vestige* (n.) means a visible trace, mark, or impression, of something absent, lost, or gone.

440. **a.** *Opportune* (adj.) means well-timed or convenient.

441. **e.** To *admonish* (v.) means to reprove kindly but seriously; to warn or counsel; to instruct or remind, as of a forgotten responsibility.

442. **d.** To *gibe* (v.) means to taunt or jeer; to utter a taunting or sarcastic remark.

443. **d.** A *realm* (n.) is a knowledge domain that you are interested in; a kingdom or domain.

444. **c.** To *exhort* (v.) means to urge strongly with a stirring argument, appeal, or advice; to make an urgent appeal.

445. **c.** *Kudos* (n.) are complimentary remarks; expressions of praise.

446. **d.** To *transgress* (v.) means to go beyond the limit or bounds of; usually in connection with a law.

447. **d.** A *girder* (n.) is a large horizontal beam, made of wood, steel, or concrete, to support weight or span an opening.

448. **d.** *Vernal* (adj.) means belonging to or suggestive of the spring.

449. **d.** *Quixotic* (adj.) means idealistic without regard for practicality.

450. **c.** *Aegis* (n.) means sponsorship or patronage; guidance or direction; or protection.

Chapter 19

451. Frank feels such _____ towards his ex-business partner that he cannot stand to be in the same room with him.

    a. iniquity

    b. collusion

    c. avarice

    d. pallor

    e. animosity

452. Ronaldo celebrated the gathering of his _____ on Thanksgiving Day and spoke with relatives he had not seen in a long time.

    a. commonwealth

    b. surrogates

    c. representatives

    d. kindred

    e. infidels

453. After sitting in the contentious board meeting for two hours, Allen's necktie began to feel like a _____ around his neck.
   a. decorum
   b. garland
   c. noose
   d. renegade
   e. monstrosity

454. Even though he hated to work holidays and weekends, Trevor hoped that his paycheck would serve as _____ for the time spent away from his family.
   a. metamorphism
   b. restitution
   c. enunciation
   d. proclamation
   e. kismet

455. Amanda's parents were shocked by her _____ decision to quit her job without notice and move to Hollywood.
   a. conscientious
   b. affable
   c. placid
   d. languid
   e. impetuous

456. The catlike movements of the sneaky _____ served him well when he picked pockets among the tourists on the crowded boardwalk.
   a. forerunner
   b. knave
   c. vigilante
   d. dignitary
   e. bureaucrat

457. The student's _____ language offended many others in the class.
   a. obsequious
   b. studious
   c. scanty
   d. surreptitious
   e. scurrilous

458. In winter, the frost on a car's windshield can be _____ to the driver.
a. lurid
b. obstructive
c. cynical
d. purified
e. salvageable

459. The prom was a _____ royal ball with so many handsome young men and beautiful young ladies dressed to the ultimate formality.
a. affable
b. virtual
c. corrosive
d. deleterious
e. inevitable

460. As the roller coaster inched to the top of the hill, Helena could feel her heart begin to _____.
a. exfoliate
b. dominate
c. reattribute
d. palpitate
e. ventilate

461. Paul's _____ humor is sometimes lost on those who take his comments too literally.
a. piquant
b. wry
c. florid
d. placid
e. negligible

462. Hearing her sister approach, Marie-Helene attempted to appear _____ as she quickly hid the birthday gift behind her back.
a. flamboyant
b. stoic
c. pivotal
d. crass
e. nonchalant

463. The knight sought to _____ his broadsword in such a menacing fashion as to frighten his attacker away.

a. warrant
b. procure
c. placate
d. wield
e. ensue

464. At the banquet, the disappearance of the woman's jeweled bracelet from her wrist appeared to be the _____ of an accomplished thief.

a. attrition
b. sledge
c. sleight
d. dismastment
e. regalia

465. Something went _____ in our experiment, and instead of creating a green odorless vapor, we ended up with a noxious red liquid that stunk up the laboratory for days.

a. hoary
b. awry
c. listless
d. derogatory
e. dilatory

466. When the movie star slipped out the back door of the hotel, the paparazzi adroitly gathered their _____ and raced around the building to catch her.

a. pandemonium
b. tenor
c. paraphernalia
d. venue
e. propaganda

467. Since Shane won the lottery, he has been living a life of _____ luxury, buying whatever he desires and traveling around the world in his 100-foot yacht as he is waited on hand and foot by a bevy of butlers, cooks, and maids.
  a. arrant
  b. vitriolic
  c. ribald
  d. seditious
  e. fatuous

468. Confronted by his mother, the _____ four-year-old could not lie about scribbling on his bedroom walls with purple and blue markers.
  a. guileless
  b. inauspicious
  c. untarnished
  d. indiscriminate
  e. vexed

469. The artist attempted to _____ the painting by adding people dressed in bright colors in the foreground.
  a. excoriate
  b. amplify
  c. eradicate
  d. vivify
  e. inculcate

470. The artist drew the picture with such _____ that it was possible to count every blade of grass that he painted.
  a. blasphemy
  b. philosophy
  c. nicety
  d. consensus
  e. purveyance

471. The highly publicized nature of the trial caused the judge to
_____ the jury in order to shield members from evidence that
might sway their verdict.
   a. quarantine
   b. retract
   c. sequester
   d. integrate
   e. assimilate

472. Jillian was _____ by the contradictory diagnoses she received and
decided she needed a third opinion.
   a. intimidated
   b. effaced
   c. girded
   d. usurped
   e. bemused

473. Because he was antsy from having eaten too much candy, little
William was unable to _____ himself in a respectable manner
during the ceremony.
   a. garner
   b. quell
   c. surmise
   d. comport
   e. subjugate

474. The chemistry professor believed her students could do better on
their exams by searching for their own answers, and encouraged
the class to apply the _____ method to prepare.
   a. punctilious
   b. nonconformist
   c. salubrious
   d. heuristic
   e. determinate

475. Bea was known for her loud and domineering personality and was
considered a _____ by many who knew her.
   a. banality
   b. debutante
   c. scapegoat
   d. trifle
   e. virago

Answers

451. **e.** *Animosity* (n.) means bitter, open hostility or enmity; energetic dislike.

452. **d.** *Kindred* (n.) is a group of people related to each other by birth or marriage.

453. **c.** A *noose* (n.) is a loop with slipknot, tightening when pulled.

454. **b.** *Restitution* (n.) is a restoration of what is lost or taken away, especially unjustly.

455. **e.** *Impetuous* (adj.) means impulsive or passionate; characterized by sudden emotion or energy.

456. **b.** *Knave* (n.) is a dishonest, deceitful, or unreliable person.

457. **e.** *Scurrilous* (adj.) means grossly indecent or vulgar; offensive.

458. **b.** *Obstructive* (adj.) means blocking, hindering; obscuring.

459. **b.** *Virtual* (adj.) means being in essence or effect, but not in actual fact.

460. **d.** To *palpitate* (v.) is to flutter or move with slight throbs.

461. **b.** *Wry* (adj.) means ironic, cynical, or sardonic.

462. **e.** *Nonchalant* (adj.) means casual, indifferent.

463. **d.** To *wield* (v.) means to use, control, or manage, as a weapon, or instrument, especially with full command.

464. **c.** A *sleight* (n.) means a trick or feat so deftly done that the manner of performance escapes observation.

465. **b.** *Awry* (adj.) means off-course, amiss; turned or twisted toward one side, askew; not functioning properly.

466. **c.** *Paraphernalia* (n.) are miscellaneous articles needed for particular professions, information, or operation.

467. **a.** *Arrant* (adj.) means complete, absolute, utter.

468. **a.** *Guileless* (adj.) means to be without guile; straightforward; honest; frank.

469. **d.** To *vivify* (v.) means to give or bring life to; to animate.

470. **c.** *Nicety* (n.) means precision, accuracy; a subtle distinction or detail; the state of being nice.

471. **c.** To *sequester* (v.) means to separate, segregate, seclude; cause to withdraw or retire, as with juries.

472. **e.** *Bemused* (adj.) means deeply absorbed in thought; bewildered or perplexed by many conflicting situations or statements.

473. **d.** To *comport* (v.) means to conduct or behave (oneself) in a certain manner; to agree, accord, or harmonize.

474. **d.** *Heuristic* (adj.) means stimulating further investigation; encouraging learning through discoveries made by a student.

475. **e.** *Virago* (n.) means a bold, impudent, turbulent woman.

Chapter 20

476. Even though he was only in kindergarten, Joel was very _____ and could intuit when his teacher was not pleased with his behavior.
   a. obtuse
   b. oblivious
   c. inept
   d. perceptive
   e. indolent

477. During his many years of hard work, Paul was promoted several times and began to rise through the bank's _____ of employees.
   a. declassification
   b. surplus
   c. hierarchy
   d. principality
   e. dominion

478. The heat was absolutely _____, making everyone irritable, sweaty, and uncomfortable.
   a. taciturn
   b. salient
   c. replete
   d. prosaic
   e. oppressive

479. The biology students were assigned the task of testing the _____, but did not have enough time to prove its validity.
   a. lexicon
   b. hypothesis
   c. motif
   d. platitude
   e. genesis

480. It had rained all afternoon, but the fans were still _____ that the baseball game would still be played.
   a. pessimistic
   b. sadistic
   c. optimistic
   d. domineering
   e. truant

481. If you have any special needs or requests, speak to Val; she's the one with the most _____ around here.
   a. synergy
   b. clout
   c. affinity
   d. guile
   e. infamy

482. Because Virgil had been so _____ as a child, he had an extremely difficult time adjusting when he enrolled in the military academy.
   a. fettered
   b. intrepid
   c. coddled
   d. pallid
   e. odious

483. Far from being a _____, Bob gets up at dawn every morning to prepare for a long day at work after which he attends classes in evening.

a. moderator
b. drone
c. replica
d. sycophant
e. sluggard

484. The vulgarity used by the football fans at the stadium was _____ and eventually lead to a penalty for the team.

a. rakish
b. quiescent
c. sagacious
d. reproachable
e. mundane

485. After the debate, Karim _____ upon many of the campaign issues in a series of detailed editorials.

a. expounded
b. ebbed
c. doffed
d. temporized
e. wrought

486. Since the judge hearing the case was related to one of the defendants, she felt she could not offer a truly _____ opinion.

a. unbiased
b. indifferent
c. unilateral
d. uninterested
e. understated

487. Abdul found his ten-hour shifts at the paper clip factory repetitive
and _____.
a. fatuous
b. nebulous
c. malleable
d. indelible
e. wearisome

488. Jonelle is a(n) _____ of the kind of student we seek: someone who
is both academically strong and actively involved in the
community.
a. paradox
b. exemplar
c. catalyst
d. mandate
e. harbinger

489. Tomas is a(n) _____ businessman who knows a good opportunity
when he sees it.
a. insolent
b. astute
c. mercurial
d. indifferent
e. volatile

490. Sean would _____ whenever it became his turn to do the dishes.
a. premeditate
b. palter
c. reform
d. distend
e. ponder

491. The barnyard scene outside the 4-H tent made a charming _____
for visitors to the state fair.
a. melee
b. tabloid
c. tableau
d. rant
e. tangent

492. The jellyfish, known for its shimmering _____, is one of nature's most intriguing creatures.
   a. resonance
   b. opulence
   c. didactics
   d. omniscience
   e. translucence

493. A decade after the _____, the members of the tribe began to drift home again, hoping to rebuild the community they had fled during the war.
   a. kowtow
   b. redaction
   c. cloister
   d. diaspora
   e. chimera

494. After performing a _____ of the cow, scientists determined that it did not have mad cow disease, and there was no need to notify the board of health.
   a. extrapolation
   b. interrogation
   c. interment
   d. elongation
   e. vivisection

495. Charged with moral _____, the judge was called off the case even though he denied receiving bribes from the plaintiff's counsel.
   a. lassitude
   b. restitution
   c. turpitude
   d. torpor
   e. vicissitude

496. I knew from Inga's _____ reply that she was offended by my question.
   a. sinuous
   b. vivacious
   c. sinister
   d. garrulous
   e. brusque

497. The cult leader's _____ obeyed his every instruction.
   a. predecessors
   b. sycophants
   c. narcissists
   d. panderers
   e. elocutionists

498. The _____wallpaper in his living room makes it difficult to find curtains and furniture that will match it.
   a. blunt
   b. fatuous
   c. verbose
   d. variegated
   e. meticulous

499. Homer's *Odyssey* was not translated into many people's _____ until after the invention of the printing press.
   a. caste
   b. epicure
   c. vernacular
   d. debutant
   e. nomenclature

500. *Don Quixote* describes the adventures of a(n) _____ knight who believes that windmills are giants and the barmaid Dulcinea is a princess.
   a. gregarious
   b. eloquent
   c. fickle
   d. errant
   e. steadfast

501. The _____ espionage plot was so sophisticated it was impossible
to believe it was the work of teenage computer hackers.
- **a.** simple
- **b.** vaporized
- **c.** byzantine
- **d.** mystical
- **e.** fusty

Answers

476. **d.** *Perceptive* (adj.) means having the ability to understand and be sensitive to.

477. **c.** *Hierarchy* (n.) is a series or system of people or things that are graded or ranked; a group of persons in authority.

478. **e.** *Oppressive* (adj.) means unreasonably burdensome; heavy.

479. **b.** *Hypothesis* (n.) is a proposition, believed to be probable, which is adopted to explain certain facts and which can be further tested.

480. **c.** *Optimistic* (adj.) means taking the most hopeful view; feeling that everything in nature is for the best.

481. **b.** *Clout* (n.) means influence, pull, or sway; power or muscle; a strike or blow, especially with the fist.

482. **c.** To *coddle* (v.) means to treat with excessive indulgence or tenderness, to baby or pamper. It also means to cook in water just below the boiling point.

483. **e.** A *sluggard* (n.) is a person who is habitually lazy or idle.

484. **a.** *Reproachable* (adj.) means needing rebuke or censure; in a manner that is severe or cutting.

485. **a.** To *expound* (v.) means to explain in detail, elaborate; to give a detailed statement or account of.

486. **a.** *Unbiased* (adj.) means completely impartial to, as in judgment.

487. **e.** *Wearisome* (adj.) means fatiguing or tiresome.

488. **b.** An *exemplar* (n.) is one who is worthy of imitation, a model or ideal; a typical or representative example.

489. **b.** *Astute* (adj.) means having or showing intelligence and shrewdness; keen, discerning.

490. **b.** To *palter* (v.) is to act insincerely; to haggle; to play tricks; equivocate.

491. **c.** A *tableau* (n.) is an arrangement of inanimate figures representing a scene from real life.

492. **e.** *Translucence* (n.) means the property or state of allowing the passage of light.

493. **d.** A *diaspora* (n.) is a dispersion of people from their original homeland, or the community formed by such a people; the dispersion of an originally homogeneous group or entity, such as a language or culture.

494. **e.** *Vivisection* (n.) means the dissection of an animal, particularly for scientific research.

495. **c.** *Turpitude* (n.) means depravity; any action that violates accepted standards.

496. **e.** *Brusque* (adj.) means abrupt, curt, or blunt in a discourteous manner.

497. **b.** A *sycophant* (n.) is a servile flatterer, especially of those in authority or influence.

498. **d.** *Variegated* (adj.) means marked with different shades or colors.

499. **c.** *Vernacular* (n.) means the language of one's country.

500. **d.** *Errant* (adj.) means wandering, roving, especially in search of adventure; straying beyond the established course or limits.

501. **c.** *Byzantine* (adj.) means highly complicated, intricate or involved; characterized by elaborate scheming and intrigue, devious; of or relating to or characteristic of the Byzantine Empire or ancient Byzantium, especially its architectural style; of or relating to the Eastern Orthodox Church.